Only in Ipswich 2013

TO JANET
BEST IPSWISHES!

[signature]

11-29-13

Doug Brendel
"The Outsidah"

Cover photos and design: Kristina Brendel
Sketches: Doug Brendel
Inspiration: The People of Ipswich, Massachusetts

ONLY IN IPSWICH 2013
© 2012 by Doug Brendel
All Rights Reserved

ISBN 978-1-300-32065-4

www.DougBrendel.com

Printed in the United States of America

For my best friend, David G. Brown, who said,
"You should move to Newburyport."

Contents, 2012

S M I T T E N

There is really not all that much difference between an obscure volunteer columnist for a humble weekly newspaper and a revered, legendary, universally acclaimed, award-inundated, magically versatile genius of an author.

Except for the tiniest twist of fate here and there

along the way, I think I could have been John Updike.

Of course I revered him. My entire adult life, I've made my living as a writer. So did he. (No, he didn't excel in writing junk mail the way I have, but he was pretty successful in his own way. Couple of Pulitzer Prizes, for example. Couple of O. Henrys. The National Medal of Arts, conferred by Congress. This sort of thing.)

And it's not widely known that Updike originally wanted to be a cartoonist. I want to be a cartoonist too! My inferior sketches all through this book attest to the fact that I have not become one. Just like Updike!

Furthermore, John Updike began his professional career writing for the *New Yorker*. By a remarkable coincidence, I began my professional career being rejected by the *New Yorker*.

Then — spookier parallels yet. John Updike famously left the magazine after only two years; I left the Arizona desert after only two decades. Updike decided to move to the very fine historic town of Ipswich, Massachusetts. I did too.

One bitter winter day, I found an antique house — hey! Updike lived in an antique house too! I would follow in The Great Man's footsteps. Almost literally. He had long since moved to a mansion down in Beverly Farms; but hey, maybe I would bump into him at Costco!

Fate spared him the embarrassment of my obsession.

He was aging, he was ill; and perhaps the universe warned him I was coming. Ten days after I signed the papers to buy my house in Ipswich, Mr. Updike slipped into eternity. He managed to dodge the fixated wannabe by a scant 250 hours. I mourned. For the world, and for myself.

Now, here, today, I confess. I want to be John Updike.

But — there are limits. Some suggest that he wrote about his Ipswich neighbors, changing names to protect the guilty. I would never stoop so high. As "The Outsidah," writing a column for the *Ipswich Chronicle*, I write about my neighbors without offering any protection whatsoever. So far, only a few people seem to despise me for it. And I have received only one direct threat. It involved a noisy rooster, which I've been warned not to write about. So I'd rather not say anything more about this. Please don't ask me about the rooster.

It is a great honor to write "The Outsidah," commenting on life in my much beloved adopted hometown from the perspective of a newcomer. Nah, *honor* is too soft a word. Updike would never settle for such a word, at least not without a page-long paragraph to go with it. But at the *Chronicle*, my esteemed editor has gently conditioned me to limit my columns to about 600 words. As I'm approaching this boundary at the moment, I'll just say it's a great honor to write "The Outsidah," and leave it at this.

I am Ipswich-besotted, and unashamed. I have made a firm commitment never to leave for a mansion in Beverly Farms. Don't try to tempt me with a Pulitzer.

Spirit of John Updike, please forgive me. For everything.

Doug Brendel
Linebrook Road

www.DougBrendel.com

January 5, 2012

You'll Need a Green Card

Ipswich isn't perfect. But we're close — so close, in fact, that I want to humbly suggest, in this New Year, a few very minor adjustments. Adjustments which might just get us from the utterly delightful 99% we are now, all the way to absolute, total perfection.

For starters, I understand we had some issues with anonymous letters last year. It's not feasible to ban anonymous letters — you don't know whom to throw in jail; that's what "anonymous" means — but I propose to impede their distribution very simply, with a new, uncomplicated town ordinance:

Article I. If you're caught giving an anonymous letter

to anyone, you have to eat it.

Article II. If you find an anonymous letter lying around — say, on an unattended counter in Town Hall — you're allowed to leave it there, or destroy it. Or, of course, if you prefer, you may eat it yourself, simply as a service to the town.

I realize there's a risk to this legislation. People may find anonymous letters tasty, and demand will increase rather than decrease. It's possible we could see the development of a black market. People writing anonymous letters just for money. Anonymous letters piccata quietly slipped out the back door at Zabaglione's, cash only. Baked anonymous letters (with mustard or without) being peddled from an unlicensed pushcart on Hammatt Street. A fried-anonymous-letter craze could threaten the clam trade.

But I feel the risk is worth it. Chances are, people will find it unpleasant to choke down all that paper and ink. Anonymous bad-mouthing undermines your spiritual health. If it also gives you heartburn, maybe it will go away.

Indeed, we all do our share of anonymous bad-mouthing. To the dogless neighbor, I snicker about the neighbor who has the noisy dog. With the neighbor who loves (and can't hear) the noisy dog, I tell myself I'm a good neighbor for smiling and pretending all is well, and hope that he will somehow get the message from someone else. I'm an old hand at cowardly neighborliness.

Long ago, I came across a simple checklist for preventing anonymous bad-mouthing and its noxious side-effects. (This checklist conforms to every major faith system I've encountered. Even atheists are OK with it.) I printed it out on a small rectangle of green card stock, and called it "The Green Card," and started giving it to people to stick up on their fridge.

You need a "green card" to work in this country, and I think we need this "Green Card" for our lives to work here in Ipswich:

The Green Card

When someone offends me, or I see or hear about wrongdoing, I will follow three guidelines:
1. Form an opinion slowly and carefully.
2. Do my best to assume the best.
3. Temper my response by reviewing my own weaknesses.

Before I say or do anything, I will ask myself three questions:
4. Have I given this enough time?
5. Do I really have all the facts?
6. Is there any way that I could be missing something, and this person really could be a victim rather than a villain?

Only IF this matter involves me AND it requires resolution, then I will:
7. Confront only the party in question.
8. Ask questions rather than issue conclusions.
9. Speak the truth in a merciful, relationship-preserving tone.

Nah, Ipswich isn't perfect. But I think getting from "delightful 99% perfect" to "all the way, absolute, total perfection" is doable. Maybe it will help to get a Green Card — and a bowl of anonymous-lettah chowdah!

THE WINTER OF OUR OUR BLEEDING DISCONTENT

It's winter. So I am going to try very hard to write, without using any bad words, a column about winter moths.

First of all, these deceptive little [bleeps] don't arrive in winter. If they were truthful, calling themselves winter moths, they would have arrived with last week's cold front, wearing little parkas and snow boots. But no. Instead, they have the audacity to appear in the hopeful, increasingly sunny, thank-God-we-survived-another-winter part of the year. At which time they immediately begin undermining the quality of life here in Ipswich. At least greenheads have the decency to go to Florida in the winter. Or somewhere.

Secondly, winter moths don't arrive as moths. They arrive as teeny little lime-colored inchworms — by the millions. Here's my Ipswich experience: Spring springs, and you set up a table and chairs under a shade umbrella in your backyard, and these wormy little so-and-so's soon blanket the seats and armrests. When you clear enough of them that you're able to sit down with a gleaming glass of your favorite ice-cold beverage, you find yourself dealing with — *Hey, what was that? Get off! Get away!* — creepy little suicide bombers jumping off the edges of the umbrella and wriggling into your hair and the creases of your T-shirt and the hinges of your sunglasses. Waiter, there's a worm in my seltzer.

But perhaps most disturbing of all is how they got up

13

in your tree in the first place.

The female winter moth has no usable wings, so the moth-babe looking for some fun can't just launch into the night sky and flutter around the nearest neon Cuervo sign. Instead, she turns your tree into a one-trunk red-light district. Maple, oak, fruit tree, or ornamental; she doesn't care. She's a loose woman, insectishly speaking.

She clings to the bark of your sugar maple and purrs seductively to the frisky boys, who are, shall we say, in full flight. The boy-moths are wearing their tiny little black leather jackets, with their hair all fuzzy the way the girls like it. They're flapping their wings, trying to look manly. Imagine a high-speed version of "I'm gonna pump — you up!" about 400 times a minute. The moth-guys are on the prowl for moth-dolls.

How long does this go on? Well, remember that long, lazy, mild autumn we enjoyed? The winter moth teenagers were partying it up the whole time. In scientific terms: *Operophtera brumata* had a longer-than-usual mating season. (Result: more winter moths this year. Oh joy.) Yes, night after night, young punk moths with tattoos on their forelegs came into your yard flapping their over-stimulated wings, found packs of equally corrupt wingless wenches hanging out looking for trouble — probably chewing gum and wearing mascara — and together, they did the unconscionable. On your property!

But then comes the real horror. (You may want to look away while you read this.) When the, uh, convergence has been converged — when the tiny little moth keg has been emptied, and tiny little moth cigarette butts are scattered among the blades of your grass — this besmirched female has to live with the consequences. She can't go home; her mother won't have her, after what she's done. (For literary types, she's Hester Prynne-sect.) So she begins to climb up your tree — pregnant, mind you, laden with regret and possibly a hangover — and high in your branches, she forlornly delivers her eggs. Soon you're landlord to hordes of little squirmers.

And does this wayward mother care for them? Does she warm 20,000 tiny baby bottles? No. She turns the ravenous little critters loose. They proceed to turn your leaves into Swiss cheese. Soon they'll be dive-bombing your backyard lemonade.

I recommend you take action. Vengeful, purposeful action.

Here's how.

On the occasional warmish winter evening, you may find a cloud of moths fluttering around a tree trunk. Now that you've read this column, you'll know: You're observing a gang of miscreant males. Sure, you could spray death from a can and kill some of them, but don't bother. The more efficient approach is to find that one blasted female on the tree itself, and send her to moth heaven or moth hell or wherever these evil creatures go when they die.

Eliminating her will also have the side-effect of torturing the males, which will be very gratifying.

And then, this spring, when the pernicious little Grinch-green tormentors reappear, take my advice: Squish away. If you have any feelings of guilt, call me. I'll preach a lovely, and entirely forgiving, moth funeral. "Dearly beloved..."

Whew! Made it. Not a single unprintable word.

January 19, 2012

THINGS YOU NEVER HAVE to SAY

I believe you have a finite number of breaths in your lifetime. It's a preset number. When you've drawn your predetermined number of breaths, it's all over for you. So when somebody says "Save your breath," don't smack them for being sarcastic. They're giving you wise advice.

In the interest of encouraging the *Chronicle*'s readers to live long and prosper, I would now like to offer a number of ways in which Ipswich residents can save their breath. What follows is a countdown of the Top Five Things You Never Have to Say.

The #5 Thing You Never Have to Say: "Is the High Street bridge finished?"

Don't waste your breath on this question. The High Street bridge, as far as I can determine, will never be finished. At least not in our lifetime. I'm relatively new to Ipswich, so of course I may not have all the details straight, but it seems to me that this project has been going on a long, long time.

No, the revamping of the High Street bridge is not, as some have sarcastically suggested, a WPA project begun during the Franklin Roosevelt administration. This project actually predates FDR, I believe. Calvin Coolidge, passing through on his way to a family reunion in Vermont, paused to say "Good job, boys" to the bridge-builders. He was speaking truth. It's a very good job. Secure, anyway.

Don't get me wrong. I'm happy for those bridge-builders. Whatever you do, don't get them mad. If they walk off the job, we're left with that thing the way it is. Bridges take time. Relax. As you creep along High Street over the railroad tracks, smile sweetly and wave gratefully to the bridge-builders. Absolutely do *not* roll down your window and shout "How much longer?" This will be a waste of breath, too.

The #4 Thing You Never Have to Say: "Things seem to be settling down at Town Hall."

You will only be periodically inclined to say this, but even when the moment seems right, don't. Sure, it may be true at the moment, but it won't be for long. And those nine non-essential words will cost you one whole breath.

Please recognize that Town Hall is a very large building which was actually designed to withstand continuous turmoil. As I understand it, at some point before I arrived in Ipswich, our government officials moved into this new facility from "Old Town Hall." Perhaps the old building was a bit too shaky for the cataclysmic conflict that Ipswich government was becoming? Anyway, I hear they're trying to turn Old Town Hall into a performing arts center — which strikes many townies as entirely appropriate, given the theatrics that happened there down through the years.

The #3 Thing You Never Have to Say: "Look! A Dunkin' Donuts!"

This is New England. We have more Dunkin' Donuts than traffic lights.

The #2 Thing You Never Have to Say: "Where do you get your ideas for your columns?"

Thank you for asking, but there's no need to ask. It's not a secret, and the truth should come as no surprise. My primary source for column ideas has been, and shall always be, the moms at the bus stop.

And the #1 Thing You Never Have to Say: "Do I need a permit for this?"

The answer is yes.

January 26, 2012

THE IPSWICH-ROWLEY WAR

Rowley invaded Ipswich.

It was perhaps inevitable. People in Ipswich, myself included, have been known to make Rowley the butt of various jokes. This is shameful behavior on our part, probably. Rowley is actually a fine town, and we need them, because we don't have a McDonald's. But still, somehow, Rowley seems to have a somewhat humorous quality. Maybe it's the name. I mention Rowley to out-of-towners and in many cases they chuckle. Isn't there just a vaguely odd, rolly-polly, puppy-clowny sound to the name "Rowley"?

I felt more or less badly about having this opinion — after all, someone whose name really was Rowley must have founded Rowley — until I learned that Rowley wasn't founded by Mr. Rowley at all. It was founded by Mr. Rogers. Not *that* Mr. Rogers. But see how humor seems to dog this town?

History tells us that Rowley was in fact founded by a certain Rev. Ezekiel Rogers, who arrived on a ship called the *John*. I think it would have been more fitting for the *John* to land at Crane Beach, which was destined to be named for a millionaire toilet-maker. But no. Rev. Rogers and his gang of 20 families got off the *John* and came to Rowley.

If you're going to start a new town, but for some reason you don't want to name it after yourself, you might decide to name it after a place you have fond memories of. Rev. Rogers, however, decided to name this new town after the place back in England that he'd gotten kicked out of. A place called, uh, Rowley.

But now, long-lost historical records, recently uncovered, seem to indicate that residents of Rowley at some point got fed up with being chuckled at. A mob, scruffy and surly, assembled at Agawam Diner with clubs and torches. Eyewitnesses claim they were muttering threatening remarks, including "They've chuckled at us for the last time" and "We're really annoyed." The rabble milled around on the Agawam parking lot for a long time, but there was still no seating available. Finally they moved down Route 1, pausing only briefly to re-supply at Winfrey's. Well stocked with penuche walnut-creams and almond butter crunch, they proceeded to the traffic light at Linebrook Road.

Their strategy was diabolically simple. They planned to seize Linebrook and effectively cut the town in two. Once they had taken control of Marini Farm, they would threaten to withhold the strawberry harvest, at which point they knew the people of Ipswich would cave in and agree to express only the highest esteem for their neighbors to the north. Rowley would finally be chuckle-free.

It might have worked, but they made the mistake of attacking on a blustery Thursday, which is garbage collection day on Linebrook Road. It was very windy, and the invaders found it impossible to advance due to a large number of rolling garbage cans in the street, and no small amount of spilled garbage blowing around. One especially strong gust sent the lid of a Rubbermaid Roughneck 20-gallon sailing like a Frisbee. It struck a Rowley woman who had just popped a Winfrey's turtlette into her mouth, causing her to swallow the entire thing without chewing. Deeply disappointed, she turned around and headed toward home — which discouraged her fellow combatants, and set in motion a general retreat. Most residents of Ipswich were unaware that an invasion had been attempted.

If these historical records are to be believed, Ipswich could be at risk of another attack. So it would probably be prudent to knock off the Rowley jokes, people.

Come on, if I can resist, so can you.

February 2, 2012

SUPER BOWL NIGHTMARE

    I was out of town on business this past weekend, in a state which shall remain nameless, and found myself, to my horror, having dinner with rabid fans of the New York Giants.

    I have a mostly ordinary existence; I have almost

never faced imminent risk of death, before this. Dinner with Giants fans! This week! I could have been poisoned, or worse.

I tried to keep my eye on the cook at all times, but the cook's spouse could easily have slipped something into a drink or slathered a bit of something invisible and deadly onto a piece of silverware. It was one of the longest nights of my life: like a Town Meeting, but without Tom Murphy.

I survived, at least physically, but the emotional toll was terrible.

I was subjected to hour after hour of snickering about the Giants ruining the Patriots' undefeated season in that nightmare Super Bowl four years ago. Deliberate mispronunciations of our coach's name (it is *not* "Bile-check," buddy; can't you *spell?*). Endless undulations of Eli worship ("He's so cute, he's so smart, he's so tough, he's so talented, he's more serious than his brother, that's why he's outlasted Peyton," on and on). I suffered waves of nausea, and not because of the overcooked New York strip.

And I was trapped, unable to fight back with the truth about Tom Brady, because my host was a much bigger guy than me, and a union member. So it would have been foolishly provocative and probably dangerous to stand up and get in his face and poke my finger into the infantile NY logo on his chest and say what I was of course thinking — that Tom Brady, as *Saturday Night Live* and YouTube have now clearly documented, is indeed the nephew of God, yea and verily. And that Tom Brady is a beacon of light in the otherwise murky world of professional sports. And that Tom Brady is a paragon of goodness, sensibility, and talent, almost entirely undiminished by his somewhat elastic views on wedding-before-pregnancy.

Giants fans are so, what's the word I'm searching for? So New York. Nothing approaching the propriety and restraint of New Englanders. Excess, wretched excess, everywhere you turn. My host not only wore a New York Giants jersey, so did his 3-year-old kid, whom he had trained to greet with an explosive "Go, Eli!" Then there was the rubber hat in the shape of a football, emblazoned with the New York Giants logo, which the kid had the audacity to plop onto my head. They had a New York Giants blanket thrown over the couch; I was forced to actually sit on it. My backside still itches.

I have not lived in Ipswich long, but my feelings about New York go way back, back to the day the Yankees squared off against the Arizona Diamondbacks in the 2001 World Series. We were all still reeling from the 9/11 attacks, and the nation's heart longed for the Yankees to rise victorious, to honor and somehow redeem the losses. We Arizona fans wanted to be sensitive to the situation, wanted to be good citizens, wanted to be, first and foremost, Americans. But there we were, unlikely neophytes, in the World Series for the first time. So when the New Yorkers came to town, we said the only thing that could be said: "Let's hate them."

It felt natural. It still does.

Stuck in the Giants fan's man-cave this past weekend, my only hope was negotiation. I offered a wager, and on that basis, they finally let me out. The deal was simple. If the Patriots lose, I get the brainwashed 3-year-old.

February 9, 2012

WHAT to THROW AWAY, and HOW

Let's see if I have this straight. About the garbage.

We're well into our second year, I believe, of the new Ipswich Garbage Law, and I am probably still a bit unclear on some details.

I think I understand the part about unlimited recycling. I confess, when I first heard the terms of the New Deal — "unlimited" recycling — my pulse quickened. "Unlimited" is a *lot* of recycling. A part of me wanted to test it, just because I could. I wanted to buy a thousand refrigerators just to put the boxes by the side of the road on Thursday morning. I *love* "unlimited"! I was restrained, however, by the lovely woman I turn all my money over to.

So: back to reality.

On Garbage & Recycling Day each week, Thursdays at my house, you can put anything curbside that's recyclable. There's one exception: Flimsy plastic cannot be recycled in Ipswich. Even though it's clearly marked as recyclable, there's a throne room somewhere, where members of the recycling royalty have passed judgment against the bag your *Boston Sunday Globe* arrives in. It is perhaps beneath the dignity of Ipswich to recycle Boston newspaper wrappers.

But let's move on. On beyond recycling, to garbage. Serious garbage. Not that wimpy recyclable stuff. Hardcore garbage. At our house, we compost everything we can — our compost heap is a turkey vulture's delight — but ultimately there's stuff you just have to throw out, as a guilty contribution to America's already bloated landfills.

And here is where it gets interesting.

Under the new Ipswich Garbage Law, I can put out one barrel of garbage — not two, like in the good old days, when candy was a penny, and Nixon was considered too liberal. Then, after I've stuffed my plastic Rubbermaid to the max, like an enormous army-green dumpling, I can buy Town-approved extra-garbage bags for $2 each, for whatever won't fit.

Yet even then, there are some items that can't be squashed into the plastic bin, and no Town bag can be stretched to cover. Under the Ipswich rubbish regs, I can still put out "one large object."

This is very generous. But it also makes me somewhat nervous.

Define *large*.

Define *object*.

"Large," I'm afraid, has its limits. And the Town's definition of "object" could be quite different from my own.

I need to replace my rickety old garage. Rather than

tearing it down, could I just drag that wretched thing to the end of the driveway some Thursday morning and find it magically gone by the end of the day? Probably not.

Good people of Ipswich, let me admonish you: If we abuse this generous, open-ended regulation, the Town fathers could easily retract it. In this situation, I believe discretion will be the better part of wisdom. Be careful about your choice of that "one large object" you station beside your garbage can.

- The rusting carcass of a long-dead John Deere tractor? No.
- The cherry tree that came down in the last big wind? Probably prohibited.
- Your mother-in-law living in the guestroom? Maybe OK. Or call dead-animal pickup.
- Your least favorite selectman? Eh, don't bother. Put them out by the side of the road, and someone driving by will figure they're being offered "free to good home." In which case, they'll simply be relocated to a place where they're appreciated. We elected these people for three years. Why let them off the hook?

February 16, 2012

THE OUTSIDAH GETS OUT

I love Ipswich, but I'm outa here.

My wife Kristina, who owns Time & Tide Fine Art in Ipswich Center, is leaving too.

And we're taking Lydia Charlotte, our fourth-grader, out of Doyon School.

We're leaving tomorrow.

Goodbye.

Wait — you could come with us. We'll be posting numerous photo reports online, the whole time we're gone.

For the next couple weeks, we'll be in the former Soviet Union, in the republic of Belarus, in the capital city of Minsk, in our apartment downtown, at #8 Karl Marx Street.

Yes, you read that right. We have an apartment on Karl Marx Street in Minsk. In the good ol' USSR.

Why? Because, in my other life — not the glamorous life of a celebrity newspaper columnist, surrounded by fawning starlets and swamped by movie offers — I lead a ministry called NewThing.net. We arrange for hundreds of tons of humanitarian aid to be delivered over the course of the year to needy people all across Belarus — in orphanages and shelters for abused and abandoned children, homes for disabled children, hospitals and clinics, prisons and juvenile detention centers, senior citizens' homes, even insane asylums.

When we're over there, as often as four times a year, we have the joy of seeing for ourselves where the aid is going, and who it's helping.

And you get to see it too, if you want.

You can visit WickedLocal.com every day and see the latest photos and news from our travels.

Why Belarus? Good question. It's Kristina's fault. First, the back story: The Chernobyl nuclear power plant exploded in 1986, the Iron Curtain fell in 1989, the Soviet Union collapsed in 1991, and by 1992 Kristina was over there shooting pictures around Chernobyl. Over the years she and her camera have repeatedly returned to the irradiated "Dead Zone" around Chernobyl, as she's documented the aftermath of the disaster. (Is this why she seems to glow? Probably.) In fact, the main body of her photographic work from the Dead Zone is now part of the permanent collection at the Chernobyl Museum in Kiev.

Along the way, over the years, Kristina fell in love with Belarus, and the Belarusians fell in love with her. Eventually she talked me into accompanying her (I hate travel; I don't even like to get out of my bathrobe) — but then I fell in love with Belarus too. And one thing led to another. Our 10-year-old Lydia Charlotte began going with us when she was 7 months old; this will be her 15th visit.

It's quite a different world from the U.S. The economy is so wrecked, average Belarusians spend nearly half their income just to put food on the table. You and I spend about 7%. Government institutions can't keep pace with the needs. So our work there is pretty important.

And it's no small miracle that we operate legally there. Some call Belarus "the last dictatorship in Europe," and the president, who came to power on the Communist Party ticket, is a fan of Josef Stalin. He's on our State Department's blacklist. They've kicked out the missionaries and the big religious charitable organizations. Yet the Belarusian government somehow seems to recognize that we mean no harm, that we just "love God and love people," as Jesus said, and that we have no other agenda. So they officially welcome us. And we gratefully return, again and again.

We'd love to have you journey with us. Bookmark the WickedLocal.com site and let the adventure begin!

(No photo reports appeared. I was shocked to be denied

an entrance visa, for the first time ever, after 12 years of work in Belarus. No official reason was given, but the Ministry of Foreign Affairs reportedly objected to my work with churches — although this is an extremely small component of my ministry in Belarus. Our NewThing.net ministry team continued attempting to gain re-entry into the country, and the Brendels were able to return to Belarus in July. To follow all the Brendels' ministry adventures, visit http://www.NewThing.net.)

February 23, 2012

Winter Gets an Icy Reception

Not enough complaining — that's my complaint.

My esteemed colleague Jamie Lee Wallace complained in these pages last week about the mild winter. I concur.

Today, once again, it's in the 40s.

Excuse me?

I came here for the bad weather.

After two decades of virtually continuous sunshine — in central Arizona, where weather forecasters commit suicide out of boredom — I happily moved to Ipswich, eagerly anticipating the atrocious New England winters.

I got here in time for last year's Snowmageddon. Awesome. I took my wimpy little electric snowblower out four times in a single day, just to keep up with the tons of icy glop falling out of that roiling gray cauldron of New England sky. I watched the street signs disappear as the snow banks rose, glowering guardians of our intersections. Intrepid Ipswich snow removal teams battled valiantly against the mocking of Mother Nature. "'Snow removal' teams?" she scoffed. "Where else can you remove it to?"

The ice dam at the edge of our roof was as thick as a fallen oak. My son and I attacked it like gladiators, with chisels and hoes, sledgehammers and blow dryers.

But this winter — well, as Jamie pointed out, we can hardly call it winter.

By King Day, my forsythia buds were swelling. I swear I heard them whistling a happy tune. In the sunshine!

This has not been a New England winter worthy of its name.

Not a single house pet has been impaled by a falling 40-pound icicle.

Not a single beaver has been frozen mid-gnaw on the Ipswich River.

Not a single child has ventured out on the ice of Hood Pond, crashed through, been rescued, and made Page 1.

No dachshund, attempting to do his business, has

been lost in a snowdrift and forced to negotiate temporary lodging with the chipmunks.

Hardly any selectmen were forced to bunk together in Town Hall because Green Street was impassible.

The Fire Department has not been called out even once to rescue a Girl Scout delivering Thin Mints on Greens Point Road whose finger was frozen to a doorbell button.

Outer Linebrook Road has never once been so slick that a driver heading west, touching his brakes at Linebrook Church, crosses himself as he passes my house, hurtling toward Old Linebrook Cemetery and finally coming to rest between Mrs. Farkis and the Poindexter clan.

Not a single tree limb on Mineral Street has been so heavy-laden with snow that it snapped off, crashing onto the head of a postal worker, scattering winter catalogs and Republican Party literature into the wind, some of which papered the windshield of a plumber's van, obscuring his vision and causing him to crash into a fire hydrant, which exploded like a geyser, showering the neighborhood with frozen droplets of Town water, quickly encasing the plumber's van and the stunned body of the postal worker in ice, and precipitously lowering the water pressure in all the homes on Mineral, leaving Mrs. Jaworski stranded in her shower with shampoo in her hair.

Knock on wood. It's only February.

March 1, 2012

CHECKPOINT CLAMMIE

I propose checkpoints.

At the town line, on every major artery, you have to clear the checkpoint.

It's like the guardhouse at Crane Beach, only it's not just for beachgoers. It's for everybody passing through our town.

If you're an Ipswich resident, you don't have to stop. You can sail on through the checkpoint with a little Ipswich resident sticker in your windshield, or a beach sticker will do. Or we'll have a little Mark of the Ipswich Beast, an invisible clam-shaped insignia laser-etched into your palm or your forehead — a little device at the checkpoint will read your insignia and cheerfully wave you on into our fine town.

The others, however, must pull over, to a special parking space, and stop.

Then, you non-Ipswich intruder, you'll have to roll down your window, and the checkpoint guard comes over to you, and subjects you to The Ipswich Driving Quiz:

1. Are you an Ipswich resident, who simply happens to be out driving around without your sticker or the Mark of the Beast? (Yes? On your way. Don't let it happen again.)

2. Have you heard of Five Corners?

3. How many corners does Five Corners actually have? (Correct answer: seven.)

4. Who has the right of way at Five Corners — Central and South Main Street drivers, North Main Street drivers, or Market Street drivers? (Deceptively simple truth: Central and South Main Street drivers always have the right of way.)

(Topsfield residents only:) 5a. What will you do after Topsfield Road turns into Market Street and you come to the stop sign at Ipswich Center? (Answer: Wait until there's an opening in traffic, then pull out.) 5b. Will you nose out into crossing traffic in an attempt to shame someone, or intimidate someone, into letting you cut in? (Correct answer: No, sir, no way, I would never do such a thing.)

6. Have you ever heard of Lord's Square?

7. Is Lord's Square really a square? (Correct answer: No, it's sort of a triangle on Quaaludes.)

8. Approaching Lord's Square from either High Street, southbound, or Central Street, northbound, where are you supposed to come to a stop? (Answer: You don't

stop.)

9. As you approach Lord's Square, when it feels like you should stop, what will you do? When you desperately want to stop at the first sharp curve, and then it feels like you *really* ought to stop at the second sharp curve, what will you do? (Correct answer: keep driving.)

10. What is likely to happen if you give in to that overpowering urge, and you stop at one of the sharp curves at Lord's Square? (Correct answer: Multiple vehicles behind me will plow into my rear end, and I will deserve it, because there are no stop signs for drivers passing through Lord's Square. There are no traffic signals. There are not even any "Slow down or you'll roll that Grand Cherokee" signs. If I stop at Lord's Square, I am committing an outrageous offense against the people of Ipswich, because I am making up a whole new traffic rule entirely on my own, and risking my life, and the lives of others, and the others are probably Ipswich residents, whose taxes are urgently needed. So no, officer, I will not stop at Lord's Square.)

Those who pass The Ipswich Driving Quiz can then continue through the checkpoint and proceed through town — unless they have New Hampshire plates. I've followed New Hampshire plates through town. In my opinion, they'll need a personal escort.

I understand these checkpoints will cost money. I am willing to fund them personally. I understand these checkpoints will require staffing. I am willing to volunteer. I understand the checkpoint guards will be loathed. I am willing to arm myself.

For the cause.

March 8, 2012

A Primer for Ye Olde Vending Tradition

Let's say you attend a Board of Selectmen's meeting, and you somehow grow weary of a citizen's query, or fatigued by a Feoffee fracas. No need to embarrass yourself by nodding off, and waking yourself with a great, loud snort. Much better to slip out into the hallway for a mood-brightening snack.

I arrived in Ipswich with a very lofty view of our selectmen, a view which, for the most part, I hold to this day. Selectmen have been solemnly governing the affairs of New England towns ever since there was a New England. So I imagined a respectfully quiet meeting room, with a long official table up front for the honorable selectmen, rows of chairs for the attending citizens. Ipswich has all of this, as it turns out.

But there's also a vending machine.

Not exactly part of my romantic historical New England town-government fantasy.

Perhaps the idea is, if you attend a Board of Selectmen's meeting, the town does not want you dropping dead of starvation, no matter how long the meeting goes. So just outside the door to the "Selectmen's Meeting Room," Room 201, there is a large, I would say imposing, vending machine.

This is not a digital-age, touch-screen, thought-activated, user-friendly device like they have at the Y. At the Y, the vending machines are totally 21st Century. There, if you're thirsty or hungry, you barely have to form the thought — "Gee, I'd sure love some Nature Valley 100% Natural Chewy Fruit & Nut Trail Mix" — before the machine takes your money, makes your change, and provides you with the snack of your dreams.

Our Board of Selectmen, on the other hand, has a vending machine of quite a different generation. This is a historic vending machine. The kind of vending machine they had in McKinley's day. Soldiers on leave from the Spanish-American War used a vending machine like this. For you to use the vending machine at Town Hall today, you will need a primer.

Here, I'll help you.

1. Note first, please, that the snacks are visible through a glass window, in nine separate compartments, top to bottom. On the right side of the machine, you'll find nine corresponding metal contraptions, each with separate slots for your nickels, dimes, and quarters. Do not be intimidated by the metal contraptions. These are simply the pieces of mechanical equipment which, in the olden days, put the "vend" in "vending machine." Fear not. You'll learn to operate this equipment in a moment. Without even needing extra insurance.

The price of the snack in each compartment is clearly indicated — and you don't even have to do the money math yourself. Cheez-Its, for example, cost 60 cents. The Cheez-Its contraption has three coin slots, each with a value indicated: 10, 25, and 25.

2. Slip your coins into the appropriate slots. For modern-era citizens now dependent on debit cards and no longer familiar with coin values: Cheez-Its require one Franklin Roosevelt and two George Washingtons. (Hold onto your Thomas Jeffersons for drinks, later.)

Take care not to slide your coins into the wrong slots. Jefferson will not fit into a Roosevelt slot, but you can lose a Roosevelt in a Washington slot forever.

3. Now comes the physical-exertion stage. Attached to each contraption there's a wheel, with a sturdy rectangular handle. Grasp the handle of the contraption in which you've placed your coins, and turn the top of the wheel away from you. Now pay attention; this is important: You must turn the wheel one full turn. If you fail to turn the wheel one full turn, the historic vending machine will take your money but refuse to give you your Cheez-Its. Any similarity with government operations is strictly coincidental.

4. Your successful turning of the wheel will presumably release your Cheez-Its from its little cage, and it will presumably plummet to the little snack-basement at the bottom of the machine. If you "push to open" the basement door, as the sign on the door advises, you will presumably find your snack lying there, only slightly the worse for wear, waiting for you to retrieve it.

(If somehow you've complied with all the requirements, but your snack doesn't appear in the little snack-basement, you're in luck: You can walk right back into the Board of Selectmen's meeting and — if it's not too late for citizens' queries — complain to your elected officials in person.)

5. If you're thirsty, there's a completely different procedure to undertake: a door to be opened, a secret compartment to be revealed, and on and on. This is an adventure worthy of Indiana Jones, instructions for which would be too lengthy to include here.

Although I have not witnessed it personally, I understand that some of our selectmen have been known to use this machine personally. I don't want to get political, so I hesitate to speculate as to which selectmen prefer which snacks. There's probably not much shame in favoring Famous Amos chocolate chip cookies, for example. But for dignity's sake, nobody wants to be the selectman who gets Snickers.

March 15, 2012

LADIES BUG ME

Please advise me.

How should I feel about these, uh, friends?

The little ones, with the orange shells, with the black spots.

Maybe my house is the only house in all of Ipswich that has the privilege of receiving these visitors. After all, here on outer Linebrook Road, we feel a bit removed. Remote. At a distance from town events. We have to cross Route 1 to get there. Some people who've lived in Ipswich all their lives think we're Boxford.

But no. We're Ipswich. We're you.

And we have your ladybugs.

It's not even officially spring yet, yet more than two weeks ago, these little — I hesitate to employ the term "buggers," but it seems appropriate — these little guys emerged from their long winter's nap.

They're in my mudroom.

They're circling the lampshade.

I attempt to fill a glass with our very fine town water from my fancy kitchen spigot, only to find a ladybug taking her morning walk over the arc of the faucet.

They're between the panes of glass in my historic windows. How do they get their bulbous orange plastic Volkswagen shells into such tiny spaces?

Yes, in seasons past, we've had the annual invasion: thousands of ladybugs clinging to the south side of the house. "Don't worry," old-time Ipswichers intone, "it happens all the time." Yeah, but it happens in October, as the critters catch their last rays before the deep freeze. This is March. This is technically still winter. This is New England. They're not supposed to be here. Not now. Not doing laps around my toilet bowl.

You hate to harm a ladybug. They seem to do no damage. They are quiet and peaceful. They seem, well, feminine. Far more feminine than if we called them *Coccinellidae*, as the scientists do — or "God's cows," as the Russians do. (Worse yet: To the Dutch, they're *Lieveheersbeestje*.)

You want to be compassionate toward them. These are not even technically bugs. They're helpful little creatures. They eat the aphids that attack our rosebushes. So we should love them.

But please. Insects should live outside. In the

summertime. Something is wrong. Something has caused this anomaly. It's global warming, or it's a Trustees of Reservations budget reduction, or it's something that will come up Monday evening during citizens' query time.

The Town of Ipswich responding firmly to my ladybug infiltration problem is not, to my way of thinking, unreasonable. Consider the big picture. Ipswich has sprayed poison into the air to kill mosquitoes. Ipswich has planted black Darth Vader boxes on the marsh to kill greenheads. Ipswich has even issued death sentences against chickens living on half-acre lots.

So I feel it would be reasonable for Ipswich to help me out with the ladybugs.

Frogs eat ladybugs. I'd like a frog grant, please.

My tax dollars at work.

March 22, 2012

GIVE ME LIBERTY OR GIVE ME ANYTHING ELSE

I've had quite a lot of unpleasant feedback to my March 1 column, suggesting that out-of-town drivers arriving at our borders should be subjected to a simple 10-question quiz before being allowed to pass through Ipswich driving enormous death-machines on wheels, otherwise known as Chevrolets, Jeeps, and BMWs.

Not that Ipswichers have questioned the wisdom of my plan. No. I have been hailed as a veritable genius, with a certain future in municipal traffic planning. Heaven knows our interim Town Manager won't be contributing to this issue; he's thrown us over in favor of Swampscott.

No, the great body of complaints about my March 1 driver-interrogation plan has come from residents of Liberty Street. They feel I haven't given *them* enough attention.

Some of these folks have not left Liberty Street since it was made a one-way.

They are still trapped there, trying to get out onto Lord's Square.

A few have escaped by turning right onto Central — 4 a.m. seems to be the best time for darting out into the flow of traffic on 133 and 1A — but those who need to cross traffic to join the northbound hordes heading toward Rowley are, for the most part, still stuck on Liberty Street.

And this is not just about turning left or right. Heaven forbid you should need to get from Liberty to Short

Street, to fill your gas tank at the Prime station or get a haircut at Detangles. Cutting across both lanes of traffic is like — well, let's just say it's a good thing that the Whittier-Porter Funeral Home is only one hard right turn and a half-mile up High Street.

Children have been born and raised on Liberty Street, have celebrated their high school graduations on Liberty Street, at grand balls thrown in their homes on Liberty Street, and are still waiting — hoping and praying — that someone will turn off of Washington Street and park in front of their house and come inside and meet them and fall in love with them and take them away to a better life.

But it never happens. Because you can't get off of Liberty Street. It's one-way.

Does anybody else find it ironic that a street called "Liberty" is the most traffic-constricted in the entire town? I dread the day someone in Ipswich town government decides that the street I live on should be renamed "Freedom Boulevard"; that's the day the Marini Farm tractors will queue up and begin an endless 20-mile-per-hour trek up and down the road formerly known as Linebrook. The Parade of Zombies.

(Shocking fact: You can calculate, simply on the basis of mathematical statistics, how long you have lived in Ipswich. The formula is simple: $A \times 3.177 = B$, where A = the number of times you've been trapped behind a farm vehicle on Linebrook Road. The value of B, then, is your years-lived-in-Ipswich.)

Please understand: I have no complaints. I love Ipswich, and I am content to leave the residents of Liberty Street trapped there. It is an opportunity for compassion. When I drop by Rite-Aid for a refill on a certain essential commodity — hearing aid batteries, perhaps, or stool softener tablets — I may take an extra few moments (if the weather is decent) to wander across the parking lot, and check in on our friends there. Our friends who are "on Liberty" but, unfortunately, not "at liberty."

"Hello, friends! How are you doing?"

And of course, they respond graciously, by honking their horns. Because they're sitting in their cars. Trying to get off of Liberty Street.

THE SILENCE OF THE SQUIRRELS

If you've ever lived anywhere besides Ipswich, as I have, then you're familiar with *Sciuridae*, the common squirrel. Like me, you had squirrels in California or Connecticut or Colorado or wherever you came here from. Here in Ipswich, we mostly have gray squirrels — *Sciurus carolinensis* — and they're so common, they're part of the landscape.

But these days, I'm afraid, something's amiss in Ipswich.

I'm talking about the astonishing spike in our number of USDs: Untimely squirrel deaths.

This is not about your everyday, run-of-the-mill squirrel deaths. Of course, squirrels die. They're not immortal. They simply — like teenagers — think of themselves as invincible. I've watched a squirrel in my own backyard, taking insane chances just to get into my backyard bird feeder — climbing the sugar maple, launching himself from an impossibly high branch, aiming

45

for the terrifyingly tiny target of a birdhouse roof, striking the pointy peak of the birdhouse with such velocity that he can't help but bounce off, scratching madly with his little claws in a desperate attempt to hang on, yet still within milliseconds plunging to the ground below, landing with a thud on the cruel New England earth. And then, yes, hopping up, looking around with a coy "I-meant-to-do-that" look, and heading back to the trunk of the sugar maple to try it all again.

I have seen squirrels going through this death-defying backyard routine again and again, yet I have never seen a squirrel die this way. Squirrels don't die in the grass, nobly, like lions felled by hunters on safari. Nor do they spend their final days in squirrel-hospice, tended by quiet, compassionate rodent-nurses. No. They die on asphalt. They get hit by Hyundais, crushed by Chryslers, flattened by Fords, mashed by Marini's tractor.

Thus it has always been.

Yet now, in Ipswich, for some reason, our Ipswich squirrels appear to be dying in record numbers.

You haven't noticed?

Sure, you find a squished squirrel on the road from time to time. This is normal. But for the past several months, I seem to find the aftermath of squirrel tragedies at every turn.

I have no official numbers from our animal control officer Matt Antczak —

he's the person you call if lost cows are blocking your driveway, or a loose horse is going door-to-door soliciting oats, or you find the corpse of a deer who had too much to drink and wandered out in front of a perfectly sober driver on Argilla Road. I imagine dead squirrels are too small-time for our animal control officer. But judging just from the number of squirrel carcasses I've come across lately, I'd say we're in a season of record-wrecking rodent ruination. Really.

Why is it happening? One can only speculate. If it's not just catastrophic coincidence — and Ipswich is being papered over by stiff squirrel fur simply because we're such lucky cusses — then what explanation can there be? Perhaps there's some new and terrible microbe in our acorns, causing our squirrels to go stupid. But I doubt it. Much likelier, I fear, that they're failing to look both ways before crossing, and we really need to offer squirrel safety classes at Town Hall. Maybe — and I trust this isn't the case — they're texting instead of paying attention to traffic.

Whatever the case, my heart breaks. For every fuzzy-tailed fellow fearlessly climbing a sugar maple and courageously dive-bombing a bird feeder, there may be another young, healthy squirrel at risk of being splattered on School Street by the Ipswich House of Pizza delivery vehicle.

I can only say to the squirrels of our town: Please, be careful. This town would be dreary without you. Here in Ipswich, let me assure you, another season of nuts awaits you.

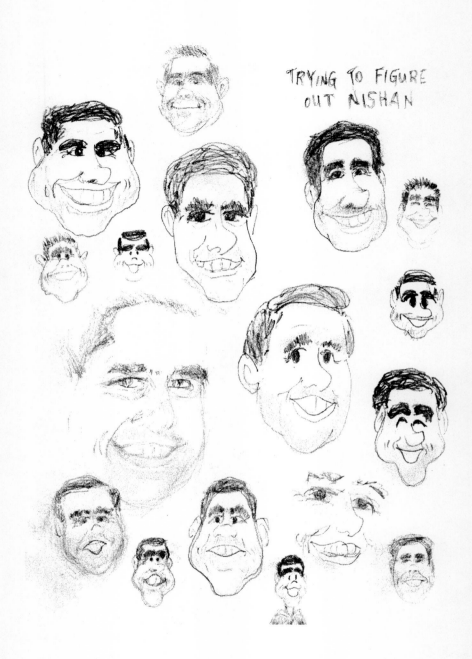

TRYING TO FIGURE
OUT NISHAN

PRIME-TIME RHYME CLIMB

This is a crisis. Two of my friends are running against each other for selectman.

It's Morley v. Mootafian. I'm very, very fond of both guys. I've done business with both of them, and happily.

I suppose it's too late to expand the Board of Selectmen to six seats, so both of my pals can play?

Nah. It's going to have to be one or the other. Let the clash commence. The rough-and-tumble of small-town politics. The agony and the ecstasy. The ceaseless march of clichés like these.

But there's something worse afoot. Worse than the anguish of choosing between my two buddies. Worse than having to make my choice and then coyly keeping it a secret. Worse than trying to stay friends with both the winner and the loser. All of this is relatively easy — compared to the struggle I'll have this December.

That's when I plan to be writing another Christmas poem for the *Chronicle*.

What Ipswich needs, at a time like this, is selectmen whose names can be easily rhymed. A McNally rally. Berry is merry. Craft laughed. Political poetry made simple!

It was already going to be a bit tricky to rhyme "chairman Ray Morley" with anything, but I was prepared to try. Now, however, there's the prospect of trying to rhyme "selectman Nishan Mootafian." This is a name to make a poet's heart tremble. I thought Charlie was going to be the greatest poetic challenge I'd ever face. (Surpitski, it's key, hits tree, quits three, wit's free — see how hard this is?)

You realize, I'm sure, that a poet has to plan ahead. Poetry doesn't just "come." Poetry has to be pondered; verse is developed, not simply delivered. A poem published in December is being noodled on, mentally, as early as April.

Which means, these days, during my morning walk, I'm muttering selectmen's rhymes to myself. Mothers push their strollers to the opposite side of the street to avoid the strange man. I confess, this whole poetry-noodling thing is not going particularly well.

"Morley, Morley. Treated poorly. Acted sorely. Jokes that floor me. Never bore me."

"Mootafian, Mootafian. Uh..."

Morley doesn't rhyme with much, but it is a common old English name. There are at least three places named Morley in the U.K. It also happens to be the fictional brand of cigarettes traditionally used in Hollywood movies and television shows, including *The Twilight Zone*, *The Outer Limits*, and *The X-Files*. In *Buffy the Vampire-Slayer*, Spike smokes Morleys. There was an episode of *The Dick Van Dyke Show* with Morley-brand chocolate cigarettes.

Mootafian, not a name familiar to many WASPs in Ipswich, is Armenian. (Armenia is that Christian country just to the east of, and often at odds with, the Muslim nation of Turkey.) For all our claims to be a diverse community — and indeed, over the centuries Ipswich has been comprised of a proud mixture of Anglo, French, Greek, Italian, and Polish folk, to name just a few of our citizens' nationalities — many of us may still arch an eyebrow when we see or hear a name as out-of-the-ordinary as "Mootafian." (For the record, here's a pronunciation key: moo-TAH-fee-un.) We're not alone in our ignorance: I searched for "Mootafian" at genealogy sites, and found even the "experts" descending into jittery heaps of gobbledygook.

Of course the Christmas poem dilemma might be solved by switching to first names. The selectmen are way easier if you only have to rhyme their first names. The challenge, however, is finding rhymes that are actually appropriate: You can't refer to snarly Charlie, shrill Bill, surly Shirley, geriatric Patrick, or halfway Ray. None of these descriptions are true. But warm-hearted Charlie, even-tempered Bill, well-mannered Shirley, youthfully energetic Patrick, and deeply committed Ray don't rhyme.

And what if we wind up electing Nishan Mootafian? I checked in with Nishan this week, to make sure I had my facts straight. He told me he probably has the most mispronounced name in town. Nishan does not rhyme with "leash on," even though many of his friends pronounce it this way. Nishan actually rhymes with "wish on." But this is still a poet's nightmare. "Wish on, fish on, dish on...."

Maybe the Christmas poem will be postponed. Till next year's selectmen's race.

And please don't tell me there's a Tiefenbacher or a Gelsomini running.

April 12, 2012

WELCOME to the TALKING HOUSE

My house in Arizona was so new, so '90s, so George H.W. Bush, so quiet. All square and fitted and plastic.

My house in Ipswich is not George Bush. It's not even Grover Cleveland. It's Adams and Monroe. Half of it was a small barn, built in 1797, the year John Adams became president. The other half is a "Federalist," built in 1817, the year James Madison retired and James Monroe took over. In each half, there's an upstairs and a downstairs, an Upper and a Lower. ("Honey, where are you?" "Upper

Monroe!")

An Adams-and-Monroe house is old, sure, but of course not very old at all by the standards of some people in this town. People who live in 1685 houses on High Street drive past my cobbled-together Colonial-and-a-cowpen and snort with derision at the white plaque hanging next to my front door. "1817! New construction! Pretender!"

My house is, however, old enough to talk. Literally. You walk through it, and it speaks to you. It creaks or grunts or giggles, depending on the condition of the wood under your feet or the threshold you're crossing. No sneaking around here. And no sleeping in, either: If someone is up and around, you hear them.

There's actually an advantage to this talkative old place: I can save money on utilities, because I don't really need *lights*. Even in the dark, the house tells you, step by step, where you are.

Let's start out back, at the breezeway door. You push, it refuses to open, you put your shoulder into it, it still refuses to open, you bang your shoulder into it, it finally gives way with a *Whump!* You step into the mudroom, and close the door behind you: *Thomp*. You rub your shoulder.

Two steps to the right — the floor says "Tecka, tecka." You pull on the kitchen door, a thin thing salvaged from the 1600s. "Weeep!" it squeaks as you open it. But then, as you close it behind you, it squeaks a different way: "Tew!"

Now you're in the kitchen, Lower Adams. The wide pine floor says *tum tum tum tum*. Turn left, and the floorboards warn you you're heading toward 1817: "Erp! Erp!" In the little walkway where Adams and Monroe meet, the floor says "Ack, ack." You know you're in the Lower Monroe living room when you hear the floor cry out like a movie damsel: "Eek!" If you have a cruel streak, you can actually bounce a little on that first floorboard and torture her: "Eek! Eek! Eek! Eek! Eek!"

Take a diagonal, cross the living room. A big braided rug under foot keeps the floor quiet: "Hm, hm, hm." But when you step off the rug again, the old pine suddenly carps at you: "Kri-ike!"

At the old, original 1817 front door, you turn left to go up a talking staircase. Each step greets you:

Ark! Wook! Pook! (Turn.)

Wah! Frack! Gleek! Wipp! Wipperipper! (Loose board, I guess.) *Bick! Kip!* (Turn.)

The last three steps are unenthusiastic: *Kruck. Toop. Bluck.*

Now you're in Upper Monroe. Turn left, and you're in the master bedroom. I can tell where I am because the floorboards mock me: "Ooh! Ook! Yeah! Wow!" Not exactly mood-setting.

Turn away from those sardonic slats, hang a right, and head into the bathroom. Flooring: black-and-white tiles, circa 1985. What's under the tile, I have no idea, but whatever it is, it screeches when you walk on it: *Reechah! Reechick! Cheekick!* Hang a left, you're on a small wooden landing connecting 1817 back to 1797. It sounds like a grandfather: "Groak. Brrp." A couple solid '70s-era steps into Upper Adams — my office, carpeted — and only here does the house go silent. Pull a U-turn and take the stairs down to Lower Adams — these steps say *Scrake, scroik, scrake, scroik* — and you're back in the kitchen.

Simple, huh?

Now let's try it with a blindfold.

April 19, 2012

CROW TABLEAU

It's clear to me that folks who have lived in Ipswich their entire lives — about 13,000 of you, it seems to me — are totally OK with the crows.

I lived in Chicago for decades. We didn't have crows in Chicago. We had pigeons. Millions of pigeons. I was in pigeon paradise.

In that city's vast public plazas — sprawling rectangles of concrete punctuated by enormous, puzzling sculptures, places where you were supposed to saunter about, or make out on park benches, or eat your sack lunch on a sunny day — pigeons, by their sheer numbers, made all of these options impossible. It was the early bird version of Occupy Wall Street. There was an immense, warbling ash-colored carpet of feathers and beaks and googly eyes, a covering so thick you could hardly walk. If you could get space on a park bench, one look at where you'd be sitting and you didn't feel like eating your lunch — Chicago is one enormous pigeon toilet — and even less like smooching your sweetie. It was pointless to wave the pigeons away: A thousand fat gray birds would erupt, flapping and gurgling and bumping into each other, only to settle back down dopily right in front of you again.

From time to time, the city fathers would proclaim a pigeon purge, but these were generally halfhearted gestures. This was Chicago, after all, which means most of those pigeons were on the rolls as Democrats, and essential on Election Day.

I lived in Phoenix for decades, too. We didn't have crows in Phoenix, either. We had roadrunners — just like the cartoon, except that in real life they're even sillier-looking. Roadrunners are incapable of walking. They can stand still, or they can jet. When they want to go somewhere, they lean forward and explode into a high-speed Groucho walk. But without the cigar. And without the mustache. Or the eyebrows, or the glasses. But other than that, it's just like Groucho.

But when I arrived in Ipswich, I didn't find multitudinous masses of pigeons, or the zigzag vapor trails of roadrunners. I did, however, find crows.

This is no measly blackbird. This is no little birdcage-sized birdie. This is a major animal. I would never want to be guilty of exaggerating, but it looks to me like a crow could easily fly off with your schnauzer. My neighbor Tanya is a black belt, but I've had crows in my backyard that I would never bet against in a round of kickboxing against her.

These are formidable fellows. They strike fear in the heart of the uninitiated. I can be in my backyard, minding my own business, when a sinister shadow falls over the land, a shadow like a 737. Then another, then another. The crows are coming. I shiver. Once they're on the ground, they survey the grounds and begin their caustic commentary. You don't have to speak crow to know what they're saying — in spite of their apparent partial deafness.

"What?" "What kind of place is this?" "What's to eat?" "What?" "I hate it here!" "So do I!" "What?" "What in the world are we wasting our time here for?" "What?" "Look at that moron!" "What?" "With the beard!" "What?" "Let's hate him!" "What?"

They stalk about the yard, glowering at the world with such disapproval, I almost feel obligated to do something different, just to seek their favor. Maybe somehow arrange a better menu for them? I normally toss out stale Meow Mix the cat refuses to eat; perhaps the crow-gods require better. Premium chipmunk cadaver-snacks? Pâté de fish guts?

To live in Ipswich, one must learn to co-exist with the crows. I am learning. I am a crow-ed student.

April 26, 2012

WHY NOT to VOTE FoR ... You KNOW

My wife, a local business owner, recently emailed three questions to each of the two gentlemen running for selectman. You can read them at Outsidah.com. These are serious questions about significant issues like schools and revenues and things that I never would have thought to ask.

My wife is a very intelligent woman, and I love her very much, and I'm not above trying to score points with her in this column. But even if I didn't love her, it seems to me that her idea is a good one: Basing our votes on straight answers by the candidates on serious questions will be way better than basing our votes on some of the issues I've heard others raising during the course of the campaign. Here's a sampling:

He hasn't been around long enough.

He's been around too long.

He's not from around here; he was born in Peabody.

He's not from around here; he was born in Lowell.

I heard him use a bad word.

He didn't return my phone call.

He has a really odd middle name. (Oh, wait — so does the other guy.)

He has a very close friend whose wife used to be in a women's league that got kicked out of that place, I can't remember its name right now, but it ended up costing the town a lot of money.

Somebody talked him into running.

He interrupted me.

I asked him a question, a very direct question, it was totally clear, and it's obvious that he didn't understand what I was asking, because his answer was, like, you know.

He gives me the creeps.

He'll be part of a majority, and that majority will lead this town to rack and ruin.

One time I was pulling into the gas station and he was pulling in from the other side and I'm sure he saw me but he just zipped right in and cut me off and I was late for spin class.

The *Chronicle* has never said anything good about him.

The *Chronicle* has never said anything bad about him.

I don't believe all that stuff I've heard about him.

I don't believe all that stuff I've heard about the other

guy.

I was on vacation in Florida, it was after 9/11, right after they let us fly again, and my brother-in-law called me, he lives in Hamilton, and it was one of those random moments when something comes up that the conversation isn't even really about, you know? And he told me what he heard about that thing, that time, when he said that, and I knew, right then, I could never vote for him for selectman, if he ran.

I've done business with him, and I really believe he made some money off of me.

I think he once looked at me out of the corner of his eye.

When he says something funny, and then he smiles, his teeth sort of go, you know.

He seems so serious.

He doesn't seem serious enough.

I look at his experience, and I say to myself, "Eh."

I used to go to the church he used to go to, and that's enough for me.

May 3, 2012

SAFE, RELATIVELY SPEAKING

Good people of Ipswich, good news: You're safe here.

And to become even safer, get into your car and hit the road.

Yes, it's official. The National Highway Traffic Safety Administration now reports that, mile for mile, you are less likely to die in a car crash in Massachusetts than anywhere else in the United States. Do not head north into New Hampshire, or south into Rhode Island, or west into New York State. Your chances of being croaked in your car go up instantly, the moment you cross the state line. And do *not* drive in Montana. Your odds of being wiped out in a car crash are 233% greater in Montana than in Massachusetts. Plus, you are 481% likelier to be finished off by a Republican.

Not that Ipswich is unsafe when you're not in your car. Ipswich is safe regardless. I have it on good authority. One of my very fine neighbors is a cop in Lawrence. One day as my police officer friend was leaving my house after a friendly visit, I made the mistake of trying to be humorous.

"I'm glad you're my neighbor," I said. "I feel safe here."

The cop just kept on walking, looking over his shoulder with a smirk.

"It's Ipswich, Doug," he snickered. "It doesn't get any safer than this."

But when you *are* in your car, here in Ipswich, on our fine, smooth roads, what might the dangers be? What exactly puts you at the most risk, when you're making a left from Brownville Avenue out onto Topsfield Road for a quick jaunt to the bar at May Flower?

Well, the government now tells us that nearly a third of all traffic fatalities are caused by drunk drivers, and very nearly as many are caused by speeders. But there's another gang of killers racing to catch up with The Drinker and The Hot-foot: The "Distracted" Driver. Yes, for every two traffic deaths caused by alcohol, there's a third caused by a cell phone. Bud Light or Blackberry, choose your weapon.

New York is the only state in the Union banning any use of a hand-held phone by a driver. Here in Massachusetts, it's only illegal to text while driving.

And it's a law routinely ignored — at least in my family:

"where r u?"

"97 home in 5"

"u r texting while u r driving!"

"bcse u r texting me while im driving!"

"stop texting me! illegal!"

"stop texting me! annoying!"

What to do? I can be terrified that my kid is barreling along Route 97 in his Hyundai, thumbing his touchscreen instead of watching the road — or I can be relieved. At least I'm home, indoors, safe from him and the drinkers and the speeders and all the other people at risk of becoming iPhontalities.

On the other hand, as I re-read these government

stats, I realize they don't account for the other awful stuff, the non-lethal stuff, that happens at the sudden, unexpectedly premature end of a road trip — like fracture, puncture, mangling, internal injury, amputation, and inconvenience.

Perhaps we're not as safe here as I thought.

Forget I said it.

Maybe I should check on my kid again.

"where r u now?"

"stop it dad im ok"

"DONT SAY U R OK WHERE R U"

"dad im in the driveway"

May 10, 2012

GET US WHILE WE'RE HOT

Regardless of who wins on Election Day next week, our town's leaders will be facing tough financial decisions. I want to help. One potential key to really putting Ipswich on the map and getting a fresh flow of revenue into this town: merchandising.

My first and best suggestion would be to sell official Board of Selectmen bobble-head dolls. The way I envision them, these are no ordinary bobble-head dolls. Some nod only up and down, others only side-to-side. And they're voice-activated: You simply speak the words, "Now it's time for citizens' queries," and they begin. For a bit more money, you can get a classic omni-directional bobble-head selectman, but with built-in audio options. While its head bobbles randomly, it can say "I don't know," "I can't really say," or "Please, please, let this meeting be over."

I feel certain these dolls will be a huge hit. I know I would certainly want the complete set of five — one for each of the four front windows of my house, and the fifth to greet you as you enter the mudroom. (I'm not saying which selectman would get the mudroom position, but I will say that this doll will be on a pedestal, under a spotlight, and I'm willing to be influenced in my choice.)

Sale of the official Ipswich Board of Selectmen bobble-head dolls will not be limited to Ipswich residents. I would expect this unique collection to be popular as far away as, say, Hamilton. If this fad catches on with the landed gentry, a Hamiltonian will hardly be able to show his face at a country club horse show anymore if he doesn't own the entire Ipswich Board of Selectmen bobble-head doll collection. Everyone will know who's "in" and who's "out" from the moment their drivers pull their Bentleys onto the parking lot at the stables. How? Because of the Ipswich Town Manager bobble-head doll with suction-cup base on their dashboards. You get it as a free bonus when you buy the whole five-selectmen collection. (We may as well make the Town Manager doll a free bonus incentive offer; we can't really charge anything for it since, for the time being, this doll actually has no head.)

I predict that sales in Hamilton will skyrocket. The money will flow into Ipswich. Soon, dear friends and neighbors, our town's money troubles will be over.

"How did you save our town, Grandpa?" our grandchildren will ask us. We'll just cackle and begin bobbling our heads.

But even if it doesn't happen — even if people don't fully appreciate my vision of Bill, Charlie, Pat, Shirley, and either Nish or Ray, all of their noble, jiggling heads gracing our window sills and office desks, our kitchen counters and bathroom shelving units — fear not. There are other possibilities. For tourists, how about an official School Committee map of Ipswich — geographically accurate, except that Little Neck is down the river.

Or we could offer official ZBA Chicken Feed: five chickens' worth per package. If you want more, it costs you $150, but as a bonus you get to spend an evening with the whole board talking about your chickens.

How about an Old Town Hall "Let's Do a Show!" kit? No end to the merchandising opportunities. We could offer Town Meeting survival gear: seat cushion, neck pillow, megaphone, ear plugs.

I'm sure you have good ideas of your own! I'm wide open to suggestions. Let me hear from you via IpsPitch@DougBrendel.com.

May 17, 2012

LIVE, FROM TOWN MEETING

(The "Annual" One)

I normally comment on life in Ipswich using words. During Town Meeting, I sketch my views in a different way. Here are my impressions from the 2012 Annual Town Meeting, misspellings and all.

379th
ANNUAL
TOWN MEETING

TOM
MURPHY
TOWN
MODERATOR

MR. NYLAND THE SEWER MAN

YOU FLUSH THE TOILET AND ... THINGS HAPPEN

MICHAEL SHAW
FIN COM

MR. HILL

67

MR. ENGEL

TOWN CLERK

WILL IT FIT IN THE FIRE STATION?

IF YOU CAN GET IT CHEAPER

INGRID MILES

FORMER CHIEF HINE

MR. McNALLY

MS SOFFRON

MR FELDMAN
ARTICLE 14
OPEB
RESOLUTION

GOVT
STUDY
COMMITTEE

MS. KLOUB

MR.
WASSERMAN

MR. GOGAN

MR.
WISTON

73

ONE, TWO, THREE STRIKES YOU'RE OUT

at the OLD TOWN MEETING

It's been more than two weeks since Town Meeting, and I'm still glowing.

Where I come from, there's no such thing as Town Meeting. In Chicago, it's unwise to get the whole town together. The last time we did it was 1968. We called it the "Democratic National Convention." There were problems.

We also never got the whole town together when I lived in Phoenix. This was simply a matter of impossible logistics. Maricopa County is literally as large as the entire state of New Hampshire. Getting to Town Meeting would be quite a trek when it's 115.

To be honest, when I first moved to Ipswich and heard about "Town Meeting," I imagined the gathering of a couple dozen high-minded gentlemen in knee-britches and powdered wigs. I thought, "How quaint, how charming." I thought, "This will be boring."

How wrong I was.

This was hundreds of people, many of them scowling, jammed into the high school auditorium. Quite a few wigs, but mostly on the elderly. Not quaint, not charming. And not a knee-britch to be found. A few of the younger punks wore shorts, but this doesn't count as Colonial gear.

And definitely not boring. Moderator Tom Murphy, like a brilliant scarecrow, chirped his warnings to the long-winded, the unfocused, and the couldn't-follow-directions types. The high-tension topics crackled, with impassioned speeches on the stage and growly questions from the floor. When it came to lackluster parliamentary stuff — "I move that the article, referring to the previous article, superseding that other article, be indefinitely postponed" — our noble leaders mercifully plowed through the fine print as quickly as humanly possible.

But for all the glamour and glory of Town Meeting, all the sensation and spectacle — with a shocking ticket price of zero, and no cover charge — I would humbly suggest that it might be possible to make some small improvements to this venerable institution. Perhaps as follows:

1. Town Meeting needs air conditioning. I believe I saw vents, and I bet they lead to ducts, which probably connect to a massive air conditioning system of some kind. I think, in those moments while the devoted citizens of Ipswich are gathering to conduct the public business of this fine town, someone "in the know" on the school maintenance staff should go right up to that massive air conditioning system and turn it on. Flip whatever switch. Push whatever button. Turn it on full blast. This way, over the course of the evening, fewer people would wilt. Those on the losing side of certain key votes might still wilt, even with the auditorium cooled to a livable temperature, but political grieving is not a problem that air conditioning can solve.

2. Town Meeting needs high-tech microphones with electric-dog-fence technology, so that when Mr. Murphy feels you've wandered off the topic long enough, he doesn't even need to interrupt you; he can just push a button on his podium, and the microphone will shoot a

bolt of electricity right into your teeth. I think Mr. Murphy demonstrated real wisdom, and great patience, at Town Meeting, and I would totally trust him to zap only those citizens who really need zapping. Also, after just the first few zaps, people would learn to think twice before they waste the town's time with semi-relevant, out-of-left-field hare-brained practically pointless goofball questions.

3. Town Meeting needs vendors. Like we had at Wrigley Field when I was young. Hot dog sellers, beer guys, roaming up and down the aisles offering their wares. Popcorn and peanuts and Cracker Jacks. How much more pleasant would it be to spend four and a half hours doing your civic duty if you could occasionally slurp an Italian ice?

I don't think these relatively minor changes would undermine the historic quality of our town, or our Town Meetings. And if these upgrades go well, we might next consider replacing those hot pink card-stock ballots. Pennants, maybe? I'm open to ideas. Feel free to sound off at Outsidah.com.

May 31, 2012

DAMPEN YOUR ENTHUSIASM

In the downpour, I couldn't quite read the new sign on my street. It was coming down so fast and furious, I had to pull my car over to the side of the road. Finally the rain subsided just enough for me to make out the wording on the sign: *WATER RESTRICTIONS — NO SPRINKLERS*.

I am new enough to Ipswich, and to life near the

coast, that I am still getting used to the water situation here. We had no little or no water in Phoenix, where I lived for more than two decades. If you look on a map of Phoenix, you will absolutely see "rivers." But if you drive onto a bridge there, park your car, step out into the brutal, blazing sunshine of the Sonoran Desert, lean over the guardrail (Don't touch it! You'll scorch your flesh!), and look down, you will see for yourself that there is absolutely no water in that so-called "river."

There is gravel.

Rivers in central Arizona are simply places where water goes on those six days a year when it rains. On these days, the newly arrived water rushes and gushes through the "river," totally bypassing the people who most urgently need it, and eventually spilling out into the Baja, where it's completely wasted on weekending California college students guzzling margaritas and mumbling, "Dude, check out that shunshet!"

We had a completely different water situation in Chicago, where I grew up. My grandparents lived half a mile from Lake Michigan. As a grownup, I lived on Lake Shore Drive; I could see the lake from my living room window. Water everywhere! But it was not the ocean. A lake by definition is an inland body of water, which means it's trapped. The rain falls in the mountains, far away, and drains down into rivers, which eventually dump into a lake. From here, the water has nowhere else to go. Think about it: the water in a lake can only sink into the muck beneath it. If there's a problem in the lake, there's really no place for it to escape to. You can swim in it if you want, and eat the fish you catch from it, but essentially it's an enormous 22,000-acre cesspool.

One year in Chicago we found thousands of dead

alewives — the fish, not the beer-drinkers' spouses — washed up on Oak Street Beach. Why did it happen? What did it mean? I think it was a cosmic message: "Verily I say unto thee, it is not natural for man to live so far from the ocean!"

At my first opportunity, I corrected this error, and repented of my sin. I moved to Ipswich. My house, in the outer limits of Ipswich, is still only eight miles from the Atlantic Ocean as the crow flies. Here in coastal New England, I thought, I would never encounter water problems, ever again. The Atlantic, after all, is 41 million square miles of water!

But then — up went the signs. Water restrictions. Lawn sprinklers banned. Garden hoses turn to satanic

serpents, agents of evil. The idea that fresh water has to fall from the skies, and mostly in New Hampshire, and then trickle down through lots of dirt and shrubbery and cigarette butts to get to us here in Massachusetts, is (frankly) somewhat repugnant to me. And we call this "fresh water"? And then it flows out into the ocean, where it somehow becomes "salt water." I'm not much of a scientist, so I don't get this at all.

But bottom line, I need someone to explain to me how we can be in a drought when it's so *moist* here. If you look closely, some of the old-time townies moaning about the rain actually have moss growing on their north sides.

Maybe when the sign says *WATER RESTRICTIONS — NO SPRINKLERS*, it just means, "Hey. Stop and think about it. Using your sprinkler in this weather would be stupid."

June 14, 2012

SHOWDOWN at the O.K. DEPOT SQUARE

Last week, I was on Depot Square, trying to turn left onto Market Street.

Sure, it can take a little while to get an opening in the traffic streaming up from Topsfield Road, especially when the train has just disgorged its commuters. But the practical reality is, eventually you will indeed make your left onto Market.

A second seems like a minute, and a minute like an hour; but the truth is, the wait for a vehicle at the Depot

Square stop sign is really very, very short. You do not need someone coming northbound to notice your plight and stop, completely busting the most basic of traffic laws, to wave you out — so that now *you* get to do something illegal and unsafe too!

Yet there I was, in my very small car, waiting patiently for a break in traffic, when some good-hearted soul did exactly this. It almost seems that some folks drive around town quivering with anticipation, hoping against hope that they'll find someone to be nice to. And here was one of them. The driver slowed, then stopped dead, giving me a warm smile and an array of hand signals, clearly urging me to embrace the innate kindness of Ipswich's drivers. Or maybe just wanting to play Pretend Traffic Cop.

I might have gone ahead and taken the left, except that at almost exactly the same moment, a southbound driver was approaching this same intersection from the north. This new vehicle was, of course, the very death-machine that right-of-way traffic laws were designed to help you avoid. If I had obeyed the Pretend Traffic Cop in the northbound car, I might have been clobbered by the southbound car.

But instead, the driver in the southbound car noticed the driver in the northbound car, and they decided to have a niceness contest. The southbound car stopped in traffic, the driver began waving his hands even more passionately, and smiling even more warmly, than the northbound driver had — while Market Street gradually clogged with vehicles.

I should have been grateful. It was a lovely moment. Neighborliness in action.

But somehow, in the face of such effusive friendliness
— I snapped.

No, I growled to myself, I am not going to pull out
and make my left turn. It's wrong. They can't make me
do it.

And I sat there.

It was not just a niceness contest; it was the Niceness Olympics. The two Good Samaritans kept gesturing, more and more vigorously, their smiles melting into scowls, and soon giving way to what surely appeared to be profanity.

But I refused to budge.

I wasn't really fighting them. I didn't make any of the gestures that came to mind in response to their finger-waggling and palm-swiping and forearm-jerking. In fact, I didn't even really look either one of them in the eye. Instead, I decided to let them learn this lesson at their own pace. I just kept sitting there. At the stop sign. Stopped. Waiting for traffic to glide by. The way it's supposed to.

I took to blithely looking around at random things — Did you realize there are 16 steps in the stone staircase on the property directly across the street? Hey, the fourth button on my radio isn't tuned to any station. Oh man, the things you learn if you look into your rearview mirror — my eyebrows really could use a trim.

What happened next still astonishes me.

I realize now that Ipswich drivers, once they've committed to suspending traffic laws in order to prove how polite they are, will not back down. They will force-feed you their goodness or kill you trying — unless they die first. This must be the same spirit that broke the back of the British Empire.

On that amazing morning, under no circumstances would either driver make the first move. I have no doubt that we might still be sitting there today, with the frustrated drivers behind them cutting new makeshift commuter routes through the Institution for Savings drive-through and the alley beside Green Grocer.

Finally, I was the one who blinked.

In a spasm of frustration and wonder, I gunned it, squealing out into the intersection and wheeling left onto Market. And feeling like a fool, of course, with dozens of drivers staring as I passed them. I, after all, was the moron who had been holding up traffic.

Hey, buddy, their glares seemed to say, *don't you know how to drive in Ipswich?*

June 21, 2012

To NECK, OR NoT to NECK

I've been hearing a lot about Little Neck. I haven't been here in Ipswich long, so when I hear about Little Neck, I still have to get my bearings. Where I came from, we didn't have Necks. We had an Arroyo Grande and an Aztec Peak and even a Bonehead Basin. But no Necks — neither Great, nor Little, nor Jeffreys.

Folks who have lived in Ipswich for years don't even think about what these terms sound like. You're "on the Neck." When we newcomers hear this, we tingle a bit. *What's on whose neck?*

It sounds to me like that old Southern spiritual, "Joshua Fit de Battle of Jericho": *Shoulder bone connected to the ... Neck bone! Neck bone connected to the ... Head bone!*

As I look at the map, it seems to me that we have a Little Neck, connected to a Great Neck, connected to Jeffreys Neck — or at least the area that Jeffreys Neck Road runs through. So that's a total of three Necks, but no heads — unless you count the Feoffees. In which case, we have two headless Necks, and one Neck that has seven.

And now, from what I've heard, our town leaders are thinking in terms of a kind of Neck brace: restricting the way people are allowed to use the Little Neck property. As I understand it, Little Neck could be officially off-limits in the winter.

This seems a shame.

I wonder if we couldn't come up with some creative uses for Little Neck during the winter months, so that Mr. William Paine's generosity doesn't go 25% to waste.

I humbly submit the following idea — recognizing, of course, that folks who have lived in Ipswich far longer will naturally have even more creative and daring notions. This is a three-part idea, and I believe it will actually solve a number of problems simultaneously.

Part 1. There's a problem with deer overrunning Great Neck. We could shoo all the deer onto Little Neck in the fall — I have a friend with a hound dog who will be happy to volunteer for this — and then put up a barricade where Little Neck Road splits into Bay and Plum Sound, to keep the deer trapped on Little Neck.

Part 2. Most of the ticks on Great Neck will naturally follow the deer. To eat the ticks, we'll need chickens —

but fortunately, Little Neck is also the ideal place to relocate our thousands of chicken-refugees, the ones forbidden to live on lots of less than an acre.

Part 3. I realize that owners of the 167 lots on Little Neck, when they return in the spring, may not prefer to live among so many deer and chickens, but this is OK. They can swap places with the folks on half-acre lots who used to own the chickens. The Little Neck folks should be delighted; they'll actually get way more land this way!

To submit variations and alternative Little Neck winter ideas, please email me via PaineOnTheNeck@DougBrendel.com. Let me hear from you by autumn!

June 28, 2012

Doctor, Doctor, Gimme the News

I have come to think of Ipswich as the place where they send mean doctors to work.

On my first checkup after I moved to town, my new doctor began ragging on me about my "numbers," my diet, my lifestyle. So I did the natural thing: I switched to another doctor. She immediately began ragging on me about my "numbers," my diet, my lifestyle. I think the doctors of Ipswich are in cahoots. And for some reason, they object to my being lazy or having any fun.

Apparently they are concerned about my coronary future. A blood test reveals that my veins are muddy with sludge, the residue of a half-century of hamburgers. Of course I wanted to know, exactly how serious is it? Well, let's put it this way: If I live another year, the town is going to allow clamming in my cholesterol.

There is also the not-so-little issue of my weight. You can tell by the narrow doors in our 195-year-old house that folks back then did not have my particular size and shape of stomach. Also, our creaky antique floorboards could give way at any moment under my ponderous poundage.

So, not long ago, I had some decisions to make:

(a) We could discreetly buttress the floorboards, but to widen all the doors would totally wreck the historical value of the house.

(b) We could call the Fire Department whenever I need to be pried out of the kitchen doorway on my way out of the living room. ("Which way would you like to go, sir? You seem to be wedged in there in the direction of the kitchen. Were you heading to the fridge again, sir?")

Or (c), least attractive option of all: I could slim down.

In response to all these subtle cues, I reluctantly changed my diet. Steamed, not fried, please. Less, not more. Oatmeal in the morning. To be truthful, the new life-cuisine is not too terrible. Still, a fresh, crunchy red bell pepper will never hold a candle to a giant, sloppy cheeseburger-with-everything at Ipswich House of Pizza. (Columnist sighs wistfully.)

But then, after dealing with the menu, there was, sad to say, the matter of exercise.

No one has ever accused me of being athletic, and the older I get, the less likely such an accusation will be. If there were an Olympic excuse-making team, I could be captain. I have a membership to the Ipswich Y, so I certainly could use the pool for exercise, but this would mean getting wet, which I abhor. (Water is something that should be observed, or sailed upon, or fished in. Don't actually lower your body into it! You're a human being, you're a land animal. Swimming is unnatural for our species. It should only be resorted to when escaping from an island prison.)

There's also a fitness room at the Y, a mirrored dungeon full of torturer's equipment. Every time I walk in there, I hear echoes of *The Princess Bride*, the six-fingered man cooing creepily to Westley: "I want you to be totally honest with me on how the machine makes you feel. This being our first try, I'll use the lowest setting." Soon, Westley is screaming.

I could take up walking, but walking is boring. Running? It's just boredom speeded-up.

So I decided to get a bicycle.

I took it out for a spin, and within the first half hour, I crashed, flinging myself at high speed into the fresh asphalt of Washington Street. When you're driving your car over it, this new asphalt feels nice and smooth. When you're scraping your flesh on it, not so much.

Fortunately, my blood was so thick with cholesterol that it oozed out of my gashes very slowly, and I didn't die.

Doctors of Ipswich, please stand by. I will probably need you again.

July 5, 2012

IT WAS A DARK and TOWNIE NIGHT

Since I love Ipswich, I've decided to think of power outages as "charming."

It was extremely rare for the electricity to shut down unexpectedly in the various places where I previously lived. Of course these were either big cities, like Chicago, with bazillions of dollars in taxes flowing into the local utilities department, or much newer, younger cities, like Phoenix, where the technology was all brand-spanking new. Or newish. Or at least post-FDR.

I have no idea what the utilities situation is in Ipswich. Maybe it's just outer Linebrook? Are we not paying our taxes? Do the power lines get funky crossing Route 1? Maybe the electrons get as far as Route 1 and stop and say to themselves, "Hey, is that really Ipswich over there? Let's go back and find out."

All I know is, for whatever reason, the lights keep going out, and if you cut power to the dishwasher mid-cycle, you can have frosted glasses without paying extra. Warning: Your drink may taste quite dishwasher-detergenty. However, if you can pitch it to your dinner guests as "Cascade cocktail," you may be able to get away with it.

At a certain frequency of power failures, it becomes wise to develop a life-strategy for dealing with them. You'll need a flashlight or two, and you'll need to do a better job than I've done of making sure the batteries are good. You'll need to remember where you stored your flashlights. By trial and error, after innumerable stubbed toes and head-bumps, I've discovered that the best place to store a flashlight is smack in the middle of the kitchen table. Someplace out in the open, where there aren't a lot of confusing, competing objects that can feel like a flashlight in the dark. It's very disappointing to find that you're trying to light your way with a can of Glade.

You also discover that your appliances, like people, have different responses to a power failure. Some simply go dark; this is the equivalent of your dad rolling over in bed and mumbling, "It's OK, go back to sleep, it'll come back on soon." Other appliances replace their clock numerals with the message "PF." This presumably stands for "Power Failure," not "Pffft!", which is the sound I imagine the Ipswich power station making at the moment the power goes off.

Other appliances blink 12:00, 12:00, 12:00, even after the power is restored, until you can't stand it anymore, and you have no choice but to reset the clock.

But the most helpful appliances are the ones that start from 00:00, when the power goes out, and begin keeping time. This tells you how long it's been since the last Ipswich power outage. On a hot night toward the end of June, we had so many power outages, it occurred to me that we were establishing a whole new system for keeping time. Forget B.C. and A.D. and B.C.E. and all that. Forget the Gregorian and Julian calendars. No need to account for the 11 days they shaved off the calendar in 1752, which goofed up George Washington's birthday. In fact, A.M. and P.M. are probably obsolete now.

What time is it? At our house, it's 09:37 S.P.O. — Since Power Outage.

No, that's not a postmodern peppermill; that's our flashlight.

July 12, 2012

IPSWICH BY PROXY

It is probably totally inappropriate to print "OMG" in a family newspaper, or maybe any newspaper — but OMG.

CNN reports that former Democratic presidential candidate John Kerry — our own dear senior Senator from the great Commonwealth of Massachusetts — "has been tapped to play Mitt Romney in debate preparations for President Barack Obama."

What does this mean?

"Kerry will mimic the presumptive GOP nominee in debate practice," the reports say, "anticipating Romney's answers and speaking style so the president can know

91

what to expect in their face-to-face showdowns this fall."

I'm speechless.

First, I'm amazed that when they thought "Who could play Romney?", and then they thought "John Kerry!", they had the nerve to ask John Kerry.

Second, the fact that Kerry was willing to do it just blows my mind.

Just asking the Senator to take on this assignment is the equivalent of screaming, "You're as boring, wooden, unnatural, pulse-deadening, and false-seeming as ... as ... as Mitt Romney!"

Please explain it to me: When Kerry's Senate staff members went to him quietly, discreetly, behind closed doors, and gently said to him, "Uh, Senator, it might be a source of, shall we say, online humor, if you were to accept this request," what was he thinking? How did he reply? Maybe "I like online humor." Or "What's *online* mean?" Or "In school we did *The Addams Family* and I played Lurch."

In any case, if this mock debate strategy works — if Kerry is superb as Romney and really gives Obama a run for his money, brilliantly tuning the President's debate performance and handing him the election — then there's no reason why we shouldn't employ the practice here in Ipswich.

• Stand-ins could be helpful in getting ready for any election, or any Town Meeting, or even just a board or committee meeting open to the public and subject to sharp exchanges between citizens and officials. Prepare by holding a mock meeting.

• Stand-ins could be employed by local business owners preparing to request permits, licenses, or any other official authorization. Set up a face-to-face, but with a substitute face on the other guy.

- Wondering how to successfully plead for the lives of your chickens on your half-acre lot? Eh, for this, you may need to stage a Shakespearean five-act play.

Act I: Mock meeting of the Board of Selectmen.

Act II: Mock ZBA hearing.

Act III: Mock visit to the Planning Office.

Act IV: Mock wrangling with the Board of Health.

Act V: Climactic final speech delivered into a microphone at a mock Town Meeting.

The only question, of course, is who plays whom?

In Act I, for example, I'm thinking celebrities. Sean Connery to play Pat McNally, Tom Cruise as Bill Craft, certainly Meryl Streep to play the part of Shirley Berry. As Nish Mootafian, of course: Donnie Osmond. If only Spencer Tracy were still alive, he could be Charlie Surpitski. In lieu of Spencer Tracy, let me check J.T. Turner's schedule.

Got better ideas? Email me via Outsidah.com.

July 26, 2012

I FLEW THROUGH THE AIR WITH THE GREATEST OF EASE

A few kind Ipswich folks have inquired about my health and well being since I reported falling off my new bicycle.

As a courtesy, I suppose I should explain.

Trying to finally get some much-needed exercise, I bought a bicycle. An ordinary blue seven-speed with

ordinary handlebars and ordinary hand brakes, nothing special except for the extra-cushy seat for my aging backside.

I had not been on a bicycle in three decades. I can now confirm that when they say "Once you learn, you never forget," it's actually just bicycle-salesperson propaganda. Sure, you may remember how to get up on two wheels, and pump your legs, and maybe even balance (although probably with an embarrassing measure of wobbling). But the folks who blithely wave their hand and say "It all comes back to you" are not accounting for how many years "it all" will have to travel in order to "come back to you."

You get onto your bicycle thinking it's going to be like it was when you were 12, and within moments you realize that your math is bad, because you've been 12 about five times over. Your joints have not been put to this kind of test since back before you encased them in calcium deposits. Each of your tendons, those once-springy little bands connecting your muscles to your bones, now bears a molecular similarity to a rubber band left out in the sun all summer. This is due to the fact that they've been lying mostly idle all these years — except for the ones in your elbows, which you have exercised many hours a day, because you use your elbows to eat and drink.

And, you soon realize, your lungs are actually flammable. In fact, they're burning your insides up — a natural defense mechanism, apparently designed by a merciful God to keep you from overdoing anything like physical exercise.

But once I got up and going, and overcame the terror I initially felt at the sound of my body creaking and wheezing, it felt grand. I sailed down Linebrook Road. I pumped my way up the hill to Marini's. I glided like a Protestant past Our Lady of Hope.

Perhaps God is a Catholic after all, because this is where the trouble began.

I took the new user-friendly corner at Washington Street, and soon encountered serious construction. To avoid it, I started to turn up Mount Pleasant, but the friendly police officer on duty kindly waved me to come ahead; a bicycle could navigate the heavy equipment and traffic barricades just fine.

However, I hadn't taken time to get well acquainted with my hand brakes. So now, in order to change direction in obedience to the policeman, I gripped them. It turns out, my brakes are really, really good. My bicycle stopped short. I didn't. In an instant, I was flying over Ipswich, like Bob Markel on Christmas Eve, except panicky.

They say your life flashes before your eyes in the instant before you die. In my case, I had enough time in the air to review not only my entire life but quite a bit of downtown real estate. I can now tell you, for example, what's on the roof at Christopher's Table.

When I finally landed, mostly on my head, the good policeman, Officer Kennedy, was quick to check on me. My helmet — which I was reluctant to wear, because it looked so stupid — had saved my brains. I took a while to catch my breath and gather my pride, sipping from a bottle of water offered by Officer Kennedy: I trust this was "my tax dollars at work"; I would feel badly if I tapped into the policeman's private stash.

Either way, I was happy to have the Ipswich Police Department on hand to confirm my survival, and to make sure I didn't need to be rushed to the hospital.

Sadly, there is no surgery for stupidity.

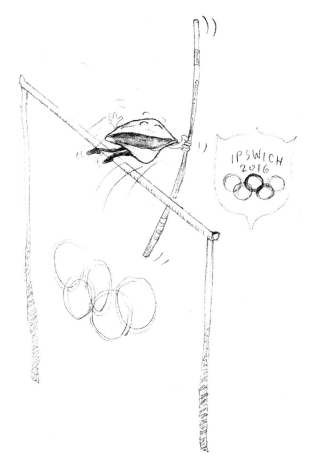

August 2, 2012

IPSWICH GOES FOR the GOLD

    The opening ceremonies of the Olympic Games absolutely thrilled me, and not just because the Queen parachuted in with James Bond. I was thrilled to realize that there are entire countries way smaller than the Town of Ipswich. Some of these countries even West Newbury could stomp on.

    On top of this, you don't have to be an actual independent country to compete in the Olympics. In the parade of "nations," we saw teams from Guam (the U.S. owns it) and the British Virgin Islands (guess who owns them), to name a couple.

What does this mean for us, here in Ipswich?

It means we can field a team in 2016.

Tuvalu — where you stop for gas, if you must, halfway between Hawaii and Australia — has less than 11,000 people, but they compete in track and field. Even Swampscott could crush them.

I think we could beat Nauru, which has fewer than 10,000 people, in judo or weightlifting, which are their two biggest Olympic sports. We have martial arts folks on Market Street; and for heavy lifting, we have the sewer pipe guys tearing up Randall Road. I would put our High Street bridge-building crew up against "St. Vincent and the Grenadines" any day.

Sorry, I can't wait. I'm going ahead on this.

Letter to the head of the International Olympic Committee:
Greetings. Please consider this request for the Town of Ipswich, Massachusetts, to be included as an official entry in the 2016 Summer Olympics. (Please designate us as "Ipswich," not "Town of Ipswich," because your Parade of Nations is alphabetically sequenced, and most of us here in Ipswich will nod off by the time you get to the M's or, at the latest, the P's.)

I strongly believe that between now and 2016, we can organize Ipswich into a number of viable teams. We have five selectmen; they are a built-in basketball squad. Charlie is awesome at center; and now that you have approved artificial limbs for Olympic competition, I am personally planning a fundraising drive to get our longest-serving selectman an Olympic-quality spring-leg. I have checked with him personally, and he is willing to do what it takes to make the team, in spite of his misgivings about the fake leg giving him an unfair advantage. Yes, I understand that in b-ball a bench is important, and alternates must be selected, but this is no problem in Ipswich: We have a large pool of former selectmen who are ready and willing to take shots.

We are also ready to compete in kayak (School Committee members will practice at Little Neck), tennis (some of Mr. Updike's old friends are still going strong), sailing (half the town is Olympic-qualified already), fencing (we are training continuously in this, in Town Meetings), and table tennis (me). We also have wrestlers with lots of experience: our two squads of Feoffees have been scrimmaging for some time.

Also, in archery, we have a number of individuals who appear to be self-trained and quite deadly. They have been practicing on Facebook and I have no doubt that they will be willing to represent Ipswich to the world, come 2016.

I look forward to receiving the good news that Ipswich will be marching in the next Summer Olympics Parade of Nations: *India ... Indonesia ... Ipswich ... Iran ... Iraq....*

Warmest regards,
Doug Brendel
P.S. Please get back to me at Outsidah.com. Thanks again.

August 9, 2012

LOVE and MONEY ACROSS the LINE

Vermont is a lovely place to visit. Vermont, you know: Green Mountains, Birkenstocks, second-least populous state in the Union. And the only state whose borders form an outline of its initial.

But there are things I don't completely understand about Vermont. For example: They say it's part of New England. This can't be quite right. It's not even one of the original 13 colonies, is it? For the record, it entered the Union in 1791. And it's landlocked. Old England is an island; no state this far from the ocean should be part of something called *New* England. I think we might allow Vermont to be designated "honorary New England," but this is as far as I can go. All in favor, say *Aye*.

There's another little issue. Vermont has now taken $100 from me.

I had the honor of being invited to officiate at my nephew's wedding this summer, but he fell for a girl who grew up in Vermont, which of course inclined her to want to be married there.

It wasn't as simple as getting in my clergymobile and driving across the border and opening my little black book and conducting the ceremony. As a clergyman residing in Massachusetts, I seem to be regarded by the state of Vermont as something of an alien. So the state of Vermont has taken steps to protect itself. There are hoops for interloper-clergy to jump through. Forms for carpetbagger-clergy to fill out.

And fees for intruder-clergy to pay.

You can get away with paying just $24, if you can get the prior approval of the "probate judge" in the town where the wedding is going to take place. This should have been simple, especially since the site of this Vermont wedding was literally a few feet inside the state line. I could have stood on the Massachusetts side and, using my Big Preacher Voice, married the happy couple as they remained standing over on the Vermont side.

But of course, this being summer, the judge was on vacation. (Probably at the Cape, don't you think?) So I moved to Plan B.

As my intrepid Ipswich attorney discovered, in Vermont you can bypass the local judge by asking the Vermont secretary of state for something called a "Request for Authorization to Officiate at a Vermont Civil Marriage." This is a very imposing document: "PLEASE PRINT CLEARLY," it booms in boldface capital letters across the top. "WRITING MUST BE LEGIBLE FOR CORRECT PROCESSING." I believe there are retired schoolteachers in a musty basement in Montpelier, huddled over stacks of these forms, clutching red pens and tsk-tsking about the irregularity of Massachusetts clergy's ascenders and descenders.

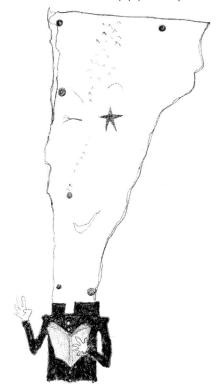

Then, at least 10 days before the ceremony, you

deliver this form to the "Vermont Secretary of State Temporary Officiant Program." Which makes you feel like a criminal, or a Star Trek droid.

You also feel strangely lighter. About $100 lighter. Yes, this filled-out form must be accompanied by $100. Otherwise it's essentially compost.

There is something wrong with this picture. If Vermonters-in-love do not find Vermont clergy entirely satisfactory, should Vermont make Massachusetts pay for this service? Perhaps every time an out-of-state clergyman is hired for a wedding in Vermont, some random member of the Vermont clergy should get a bill in the mail for $100.

Sad to say, however, hiring a Massachusetts clergyman is no guarantee of a good wedding. I did a very bad job of officiating at my nephew's ceremony.

But I swear, it was accidental. It had nothing to do with begrudging the hundred bucks. I promise. I mean it. Really.

August 16, 2012

HOME IS WHERE the CRIME IS

I feel badly that Robin Crosbie, our new Town Manager, arrived to start her new job just as all of Ipswich was being shocked and rocked by a massive crime wave. Well, not exactly all of Ipswich; mostly just outer Linebrook. Actually just the vicinity of Randall Road. Or to be precise: my house.

And I guess I shouldn't refer to it as a "massive" crime wave. Maybe "wave" isn't right either. I can't really be sure about the "crime" part, to tell you the truth.

But I do know this much: My garbage can is missing.

In the relatively short time I've lived in Ipswich, I've gathered that we don't really seem to have a serious crime problem. The police log in the weekly *Chronicle* is mostly entertaining. People sometimes seem to lose stuff if they don't lock their cars. There's the occasional out-of-control daughter and the intermittent loose cow, but these aren't criminals. Especially not the cow.

Yet when I arrived at my home on Thursday, garbage pickup day in my neighborhood, I found myself at the scene of a crime — either this, or I had just missed the Garbage Can Rapture. Yes, my garbage was gone, as usual. But the garbage can I'd left it in was gone too.

It was a standard-issue 32-gallon garbage can, not a specialty garbage can or a collector's item, not a vintage garbage can or a garbage can signed by a movie star. I don't believe "The Outsidah" has any fans crazed enough to steal the columnist's garbage, let alone his garbage can; and just to make sure, I never did glue a big photo of myself to the side of it.

Still, someone seems to have decided that my garbage can — of all the garbage cans in Ipswich — was pilfer-worthy.

It's possible that this incident was the result of a particular brand of road rage. Perhaps after our fine Ipswich garbage collectors emptied my Rubbermaid Roughneck, they sent the lid sailing like a Frisbee — inadvertently, I'm sure — and the can itself rolling down Linebrook Road — unintentionally, I have no doubt. Then, perhaps one or more drivers, guiding their vehicles through our 25 mph neighborhood, doing about 40, had to dodge my garbage can as it lolled about on the asphalt. Perhaps someone had anger management issues, and stopped their vehicle, and got out, and chased my rolling garbage can, and caught it, and dragged it back to their car, and stuffed it into the back seat, and proceeded to drive red-faced, huffing and puffing and muttering curses, toward their intended destination.

I'm no police detective; I don't know how the crime was committed. All I know is that I came to be, in the earliest days of the Robin Crosbie regime, the victim of a senseless crime.

We tend to pin our hopes on a new leader, and of course this can lead to disappointment. Some folks seem to be a little disenchanted with President Obama, for example. A certain number of Massachusetts residents seem ready to throw Scott Brown under the Elizabeth Warren bus. When Ms. Crosbie arrived to take over the helm of our fine town, it never occurred to me that her new Administration would be associated with such an upsurge in lawlessness over such a broad swath of Ipswich, stretching from my mailbox all the way over to my honey locust.

Not that I blame the new Town Manager. Not at all. I like her. I met her briefly last week, when our paths happened to cross. Criminals are perhaps taking unfair advantage, sneakily striking while the new TM is still getting her bearings, still getting moved in, still figuring out what she needs for her condo. Like a garbage can, maybe.

Wait, no — I don't mean to suggest there's any correlation whatsoever between the arrival of the new Town Manager and the virtually simultaneous disappearance of, uh...

On the other hand, if you happen to get invited over

to her place, look around a bit and see if she has a dark green 32-pound Rubbermaid Roughneck, the kind with a matching green lid — also, check for a series of blackish scratches under one handle, where I accidentally crashed my Honda into it in the garage.

And then let me know.

August 23, 2012

MYSTERY SOLVED: THE BUTLER DIDN'T DO IT

We're living in confusing times. At least on outer Linebrook Road.

In these pages last week, I reported on the mysterious theft of my garbage can. Some felt it was unwise of me to point out the fact that our new Town Manager, Robin Crosbie, arrived in Ipswich at almost the same moment my garbage can went missing, since it was almost certainly a total coincidence, and no one actually saw her take it.

Why, my friends asked, why would you risk inciting the ire of our new master, especially if she turns out to be one of the most insidious criminal minds of the century?

However, I am as fearless as I am feckless. So I went ahead and laid out, in this column last week, all the suspicious aspects of the garbage can heist.

And then came the facts. Those pesky, pesky facts.

To review the origins of the case, we must go back in time, all the way to Garbage Pickup Day, two Thursdays ago. And we must cross the street, to the home of my good neighbor, who is also my plumber. He is married to a worker in my dentist's office. The plot thickens.

When the plumber comes home after a long, hard day of plumbing, his wife has already come home from a long, hard day of dental officing. He cannot help but notice a troubled look on his wife's face.

"I could have sworn I brought the garbage can in," she says. "But when I got home, it was out there at the street, with the lid on."

The plumber shrugs. Dragging the empty garbage can back into the garage on Thursday afternoon isn't on his list of chores in this marriage, so what does he care?

Time passes. A week goes by. On the following Thursday morning, the plumber stops at Cumberland Farms, as usual, to read the *Chronicle*. He finds "The Outsidah" ranting about a missing garbage can. He frowns at the columnist's suggestions. He is growing suspicious of the suspicions.

At the end of his workday, he again returns home. He confronts his wife.

"How many garbage cans do we own?" he demands.

"One," she replies innocently.

The plumber stalks to his garage, opens the door, and scowls into the gloom. There, among the rakes and shovels, between the lawnmower and the weed-whacker, he discovers the truth.

His dental-office worker wife has become an unwitting garbage can thief.

And the new Town Manager is taking the rap.

All because the garbage collectors returned my garbage can to the wrong side of the street.

I had a visit from my plumber-neighbor yesterday. He confessed to the crime, on behalf of his wife, who is hiding out somewhere, hoping not to be hauled in to Ipswich Garbage Court and prosecuted to the full extent of the law. He returned the missing property.

Unfortunately, I had already gone to Tedford's and bought a replacement. This means I now own twice as many garbage cans as Ipswich will allow me to put out legally. Another example of how one crime leads to another, and neighborhoods decline.

I visited Town Hall and left a bouquet of flowers for the wrongly suspected Town Manager. I only hope I haven't destroyed her career in public service.

And for my good neighbor the plumber, who honorably ratted on his own wife, I'm buying a subscription to the *Chronicle*.

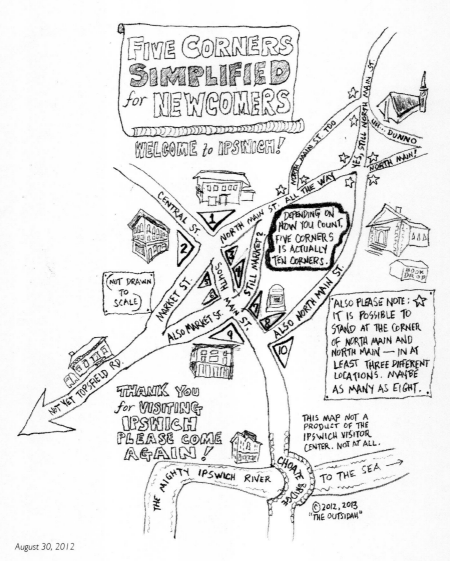

Five Corners Simplified for Newcomers

WELCOME to IPSWICH!

CENTRAL ST.

NORTH MAIN ST. ALL THE WAY

NORTH MAIN ST. TOO

YES, STILL NORTH MAIN ST.

UH... DUNNO

NORTH MAIN!

MARKET ST.

SOUTH MAIN ST.

STILL MARKET 2.

ALSO MARKET ST.

ALSO NORTH MAIN ST.

NOT YET TOPSFIELD RD.

1 2 3 4 5 6 7 8 9 10

DEPENDING ON HOW YOU COUNT, FIVE CORNERS IS ACTUALLY TEN CORNERS.

(NOT DRAWN TO SCALE)

BOOK DROP

ALSO PLEASE NOTE: IT IS POSSIBLE TO STAND AT THE CORNER OF NORTH MAIN AND NORTH MAIN — IN AT LEAST THREE DIFFERENT LOCATIONS. MAYBE AS MANY AS EIGHT.

THANK YOU for VISITING IPSWICH PLEASE COME AGAIN!

THIS MAP NOT A PRODUCT OF THE IPSWICH VISITOR CENTER. NOT AT ALL.

THE MIGHTY IPSWICH RIVER

CHOATE BRIDGE

TO THE SEA →

© 2012, 2013 "THE OUTSIDAH"

August 30, 2012

STOP ME BEFORE I DO IT AGAIN

I am really, really trying to quit.

Beginning with the very first column I ever wrote for this newspaper, I have commented more or less continuously on the traffic in Ipswich. I'm trying to give it up, but it's so, so hard.

I've never said that our traffic is bad. It's not heavy traffic. It's not Boston traffic. It's — what is the word? — idiosyncratic. It is, shall we say, interesting in its Ipswichiosity.

My personal history as a driver of automobiles in other cities did not prepare me well for the anomalies of Ipswich traffic. In Chicago, they run you over. In Boston, they cut you off. In Maricopa County, Arizona, which is literally as large as the entire state of New Hampshire, it's just one massive movie-car-chase scene, because wherever you're going, you've got so much ground to cover, if you don't go 90, you'll never get there.

Ipswich traffic is different. It's friendly. It's so nice, so neighborly, so *prudent* ... well, I may need therapy to live here. Maybe I'm just deranged by all those years in the Big City, playing real-life bumper cars with the death machine operators.

I have tried the 12-step program Columnists Anonymous, but I have never been able to get past Step 1: "I admit that I'm powerless over my addiction" — in this case, writing about Ipswich traffic. I can't bring myself to believe, deep down inside, that I'm actually powerless — that I can't somehow make things different.

Yes, I realize I'm new in town, and I can't have even the slightest influence until at least 2029. I realize these rolling roads, stripes of asphalt laid over the paths trod by cows of the Colonial era, were not laid out by mere human hands — God Himself directed the design, as He guided the Colonial cows to wander hither and yon. I think it was sort of a cosmic doodling exercise. Perhaps God was having a slow day. Perhaps he was a little bored, waiting for someone to invent Words With

Friends. Perhaps His traffic-management angels somehow missed foreseeing the poor lady from Swampscott who spent two and a half weeks stranded in her Subaru, paralyzed with fear and confusion at that little triangle of grass where County Street, South Main Street, Poplar Street, and South Village Green all come together. I've spent time there myself, pondering great truths like "Who really has the right-of-way here?"

But every time I swear I'll never write another column about Ipswich traffic, I find myself sitting behind the wheel in the midst of yet another Nightmare on Elm Street, or Hallucination on High Street, and the urge within me begins to throb anew: *Write, Doug! Write about the traffic!*

I am really trying to quit. But not hard enough. I can't quit. Not here, in a town that sports not only the enigma of Lord's Square (with the High Street stop sign bonus feature) — and the Five Corners conundrum — plus the Town Farm–High Street Bridge puzzle — but also the Hammatt–Depot Square–Washington Street train crossing thingy-doodle which, on Google Earth, looks like a warped wishbone.

For a traffic-obsessed columnist, Ipswich is just too tempting.

Like, have you tried coming east from Marini on Linebrook Road, and then when you get to — oh, never mind. I'll write about it next time.

September 6, 2012

DEER, ME

So I said to the deer, in my backyard, "You OK?"
It was only a courtesy, on my part. She looked entirely
OK to me. Like all the other deer who frequent my
backyard. Well fed. They eat the hostas in my garden.

There seem to be enough hostas in my garden to supply the entire outer Linebrook deer population on an annual basis. The hostas keep coming up, the deer keep eating them, and I have yet to find a deer dead of malnutrition in my backyard.

This deer seemed comfortable. Not nervous at all. I think they know by now that I won't take action against them, even though they don't legally have any claim to my property. (At one point I tried to take a doe to court to share a portion of my tax burden, but her clever lawyer used that weepy "Bambi defense," and I didn't have a chance with the jury.)

So I tried to be casual, and friendly, with this deer. She was lounging at my backyard pub table, under my umbrella. Sitting on one of my bar stools, with one of her hooves propped up on the next stool. Her fat, hosta-stuffed belly was protruding unpleasantly. But was I going to comment on this? No. I'm trying to be a good neighbor.

"You OK?" I asked her.

She looked at me with that look. You know, that look that deer give you. I don't mean that "deer-in-the-headlights" look, because this was about 5 p.m. so it wasn't even dark. No. She was giving me that other look. It's the look that deer give you when you encounter them in broad daylight. They sort of lower their eyelids and seem to give you a sneer. They look at you as if to say, "What are *you* doing here? You're a nuisance. Your very presence forces me to put my annoying hair-trigger nervous system on alert. Why don't you just go away?"

You know this look. If you have a teenage daughter, you certainly know this look.

"You OK?" I asked the deer.

She leaned back sullenly on the bar stool, tapping her cigarette into an ashtray on my pub table.

"Don't like that sign," she muttered.

"What sign?" I asked.

She cocked her head toward Lillian Drive.

"Deer Crossing," she rasped, and took a drag on her Virginia Slim.

I know the sign well. Yellow, diamond-shaped. Silhouette of a deer jumping across Linebrook Road.

"You have a problem with the sign?" I asked her.

She sighed heavily and took another swig of her Budweiser.

"I don't like where they make us cross," she finally grumbled.

I didn't know what to say.

"Why do you think cars keep hitting deer?" she demanded. "Because they make us cross at the worst possible places." She crushed her butt. "I've lost three cousins on Linebrook Road alone. Every one of them was crossing legally, right at the sign."

She looked away.

I took a breath. "I think they put the signs up where the deer *want* to cross," I ventured weakly.

The doe snorted. "Sure they do," she grunted. "You think I don't want to cross at the light? But no. Ipswich has me crossing in the kill zone. Thanks."

She drained her Bud.

"Thanks a lot."

I gulped.

"This town is hell for deer," she murmured.

She swung her leg down and stood up from the chair. "Gotta go," she said, heading toward the road without looking back. "Rush hour. Wish me luck."

September 13, 2012

MIGHT AS WELL FACE It, You'RE ADDICTED to MEETING

I'm ready.

Bring it on, baby.

Town Meeting, here I come.

Tom Murphy, our very fine Town Moderator, has recently advised us, in these pages, that Town Meeting is coming, and we should get ready for it, and I'm telling you, I am so ready.

My heart rejoiceth.

Oh, this venerable tradition, unchanged for centuries, yet ever-shifting, ever-new!

Oh, this link to our past, by which we lay claim to our future!

Oh, this inspiration for overwrought poetry!

Of course, I'm new around here, so I understand I don't get all the nuances.

I realize not everyone in Ipswich was happy with the suggestions for Town Meeting that I previously offered in these pages. Some felt it was disrespectful to consider selling Town Meeting survival gear: seat cushions, neck pillows, megaphones, ear plugs.

I'm afraid these same folks are probably not going to like my new idea: a kiosk in the lobby offering cake, candles, and pointy hats for those who grow a year older before the meeting is over.

Certainly there are people who feel Town Meeting is fine as it is. I respect this. Some of these folks have lived here since 1633. Think of the cumulative total number of years they've spent in Town Meetings, and you must agree that they deserve to have their say. I admire them. I am a big fan of Town Meeting. It is a venerable and valuable tradition. I think every Ipswich citizen should attend.

In fact, I think we should return to the 1643 by-law imposing a one-shilling fine on non-attenders. Of course shillings are hard to come by these days; so as a courtesy, I'd like to have a booth out on the parking lot, where you can buy a shilling for five bucks.

Or maybe we should offer a carrot rather than a stick. Instead of the one-shilling fine, let's set up a cash bar in the lobby.

Plus, the YMCA can have a "wellness booth" where they offer energy bars for the weary. And sedatives for the obstreperous.

Town Meeting is worth tinkering with, because there will always be Town Meetings. As Moderator Murphy explained in his recent column, an annual Town Meeting is required by state law. I guess if you don't hold one, you get kicked out of the Commonwealth. Perhaps some folks really hate Town Meetings, but they attend faithfully just to keep Ipswich from being deported to New Hampshire. It's one thing to spend six hours of your life stuck in Town Meeting; it's quite another to spend the other 364 days and 18 hours in New Hampshire.

On the other hand, I suspect there are some folks who love Town Meeting too much. While our Ipswich by-laws require the state-mandated annual Town Meeting to be held on the second Tuesday in May, adding a second "special" Town Meeting in October may actually be enabling people who are struggling with a tragic Town Meeting addiction. These are people who keep their rectangular Day-Glo Town Meeting ballots as mementoes. These are people who download the video from ICAM and keep all the Town Meetings in their personal DVD collection. They don't need another Town Meeting. They need help. Maybe we could give them a step-down meeting. Maybe a seat on the Government Study Committee.

But until we vote them the help they need — which of course will require more Warrants, and Articles, and other stuff I'll need the Murpherator to explain to me — I'm going to be there. Front row. Every Town Meeting. No matter how many we have. Meet monthly, I don't care. Bring it. I'm there. Kept my Day-Glo ballot from the last Town Meeting. I'm ready to vote.

September 20, 2012

SUMMER SCUM, and SUMMERS GO

An acquaintance of mine, not long ago, was howling — well, to be honest, you can't quite tell on Facebook whether someone is howling, growling, wailing, whining, screaming, roaring, or simply muttering; but it seemed to me she was unhappy.

It was the thick of summer — at least it seemed this way to me: soupy humidity sliming my skin, sunshine sizzling on your eyeballs, even the mosquitoes moaning in the heat.

But my friend was bemoaning the end of summer.

The shadows, she claimed, were lengthening sooner,

and depressing her. The days, she observed, were getting shorter, and she was feeling that stomach-clutching sadness that grabs you when you realize something bad and inevitable is closing in on you.

On the other hand, this was August. Puh-leeze! Yes, technically, I guess, the days start getting shorter in the third week of June, but come on. A neighbor's plastic lawn chairs were melting. My asphalt driveway was gooey, gliding like a glacier, in slow motion, toward the sultry street.

What I mean is, it was hot.

And then, by a twist of fate, I observed the closing days of summer with a brief trip to the hottest city in America: Phoenix, Arizona. This is not the right time of year to visit the Great Sonoran Desert, the vast sandbox which Phoenix is plopped down in the middle of. But business required that I be there, so my wife pushed me out of my house, pried my fingers from the door frame, stuffed a sock in my mouth to muffle my screams, strapped me into a seatbelt and shoulder harness, force-fed me a handful of Ambien, took me to Logan, and put me on an airplane.

When I stumbled off the jetway and into the familiar expanses of Sky Harbor International Airport — this was my hometown airport for more than two decades — my internal thermometer started clicking insanely, like a Geiger counter. Strangely, the people of Phoenix were all cheery, bright-eyed, rejoicing. Why? Because the temperature had just the day before finally dropped below 100 Fahrenheit. I almost shivered at the news.

Soon, however, I was free to flee, back to dear, chilly New England. Today, I have returned to the safety of my quirky old house, where you can see through the floorboards into my beloved dirt-floor basement, where it's a constant 69 degrees. I can breathe again. Hope is in sight. This Saturday, September 22, is the official first day of autumn.

Good people of Ipswich, verily I say unto thee, as summer slips away: This is no time for weeping and gnashing of teeth. This is cause for celebration. Fall is why we live in New England. Trees flaring, gorgeous. Pumpkins plumping proudly in the patch. A certain crispness in the air, nicely aligned with a certain crispness in the townies. We set our face like a flint toward the onset of winter. We brace for the frigid, bone-snapping winds, the great globs of slush in the gutter, the moaning of the eaves under punishing mammoth mountains of snow. Salt and sand grinding under your soles into the obstinate ice. Bare trees skinny and spindly, shivering in their sleep.

See what we have to look forward to?
I love this time of year.
Summer 2012, R.I.P.
And good riddance.

September 27, 2012

YOUR HUSBAND Is/Isn't DISGUSTING

Halloween approacheth. A time for the grim and the gruesome. The creepy and the crawly. Also preschoolers in Iron Man underwear with plastic Sponge Bob trick-or-treat buckets.

In our outer Linebrook neighborhood, we're doing Halloween right this year. We've brought in the creepiest Halloween feature of all: rats. Not children in rat costumes. Not rubber-rat squeeze toys, or fuzzy stuffed rat toys laced with catnip for your tabby. No, we're talking actual rats.

There go my property values.

There is nothing like a letter from the Board of Health to set your Halloween season in motion a full month early. Mine arrived recently with the following ghoulish news: "The Health Office has received two calls from residents" in our neighborhood "regarding the presence of rats on their properties."

My initial, visceral response was, of course, denial. These residents, in complaining about "rats," must have been referring to wayward husbands. Maybe even just lazy husbands. The first half-page of the letter was chock full of "Look for Evidence" tips, and you can easily see how they might refer to husbands: "Droppings may be found near shelter." "Tracks, including footprints, may be seen in mud." "Sounds, such as gnawing, are common." Husbands. Yes.

"Walk around after dark with a flashlight," the Board of Health recommends. "This will help you see where rats are going." I would add, Get in your car and follow him. It's possible he's just headed for an innocent drink at a downtown bar.

And how to deal with your husband problem, er, rat problem?

"Clutter gives rats lots of places to sleep." I never thought of it this way. But it's true. Especially during football season, a mini-mountain range of football-watching stuff accumulates around the couch — as the Board of Health puts it, "Fresh accumulations of gnawed material indicate active infestations" — and as the season continues, the couch somehow becomes more and more inviting as a sleeping place. Look, I have, right here at my fingertips, my Cheetos and my six-pack and my Tums. And the Pats are playing. And afterward, you know, they'll play again, in only a week. It seems foolish to go to all the effort of standing up and climbing all the way upstairs to bed.

The Board of Health also recommends that you "clean out your basement and yard." It seems to me, if your husband is a rat, he is not going to do this for you.

Eventually, however, if you read the Board of Health letter with anything like an open mind, you have to realize that it's probably not about husbands. These are actual rats they're talking about. With greasy hair and beady little eyes and a willingness to gorge themselves on just about any junk that happens to be available.

Wait. Maybe I should distinguish from husbands even further. OK, let's try this: A rat has teeth like razors and claws like needles. Devil's ears. A long fleshy tail. It's like he's wearing a nauseating Halloween costume; he just can't take it off.

So now that the Ipswich Board of Health has advised us we have rats living in our neighborhood — freeloading, I might add, since they have yet to pay a penny in property taxes — our household has committed to an all-out rodent counter-offensive. We will do as the Board of Health recommends. We will clear out our junk. We will rework our firewood-stacking strategy. Most painful of all, we will cease adding to our compost heap — a beautiful hodgepodge of gradually decomposing organic stuff, big enough for astronauts orbiting the earth to take snapshots of. Henceforth, we'll reluctantly employ a totally enclosed compost system, utterly airtight, utterly modern, utterly unworthy of

Abigail Adams and the history of the Commonwealth.

Halloween night, when your doorbell rings, and someone says "Trick or treat!", but it doesn't sound quite like a child ... if it sounds like the late Paul Lynde, voicing the role of Templeton the Rat in the movie version of *Charlotte's Web* ... or if it sounds like the actual gnawing of the actual teeth of an actual rodent ... don't open the door.

On the other hand, if it's your husband, let him in. Forgive him. He was only being himself.

October 11, 2012

CHICKEN LADY MORPHS INto Cow LADY

Some people have all the luck.

Like the Chicken Lady, for example.

You already realize, I'm sure, at the very mention of the Chicken Lady, that what follows will not be the usual lighthearted "Outsidah" column, wavering as always between the merely obnoxious and the patently offensive. No. This is going to be hard news.

I am not accustomed to reporting the news in this column. The *Chronicle* has hard-working reporters reporting the news every day, and I salute them. But this story, a story of great potential public interest, seems to have slipped through the cracks this past spring, and as a public service I now bring it to these pages for your consideration.

The Chicken Lady, you'll recall, is a longsuffering citizen, resident of a half-acre lot on Lakemans Lane, whose six chickens came under fire from the Town of Ipswich last year. Trying to get her poultry legalized, she dutifully put in her time with the Zoning Board of Appeals, the Board of Selectmen, the Board of Health, and the nonprofit group Legroom for Poultry. (In fact, at our upcoming Town Meeting, you may have an opportunity to vote "yes" to ease the regulatory stranglehold on her chickens, and all Ipswich chickens, a stranglehold which, of course, the Creator never designed chickens to endure.)

After all the meetings, hearings, interrogations, and other indignities the Chicken Lady has been obliged to undergo, one might expect the universe to give her a break. But no.

It was Mother's Day. The Chicken Lady was looking forward to sleeping in. Her husband was committed to doing the family's standard "morning chicken duty" — you let the chickens out of their coop and into the yard, to stretch their drumsticks, then you scatter some fowl-friendly breakfast seed for the pets to peck — so his dear wife could stay in bed.

But it was not to be.

The Chicken Lady was roused from her slumber by early morning noises. Not chickens pleasantly clucking. Not little daughters giggling while making breakfast for Mommy. No.

It was mooing.

Imagining she was hearing mooing, the Chicken Lady flopped over grumpily in bed. She couldn't have just heard mooing. They own chickens, not — you know — mammals. In a moment, she was relaxing, ready to slip back into dreamland. But then: *Moo*. The Chicken Lady blinked and stared at the ceiling. She lay still and listened.

Silence.

Then — there it was again: *Moo.*

She pulled the pillow over her head. *Moo. Moo. Mooooo.* The pillow was ineffective. *Moooooooo.* Then came the police sirens, far-off in the distance at first, but blaring more and more loudly by the second. Then came the crashes, metal and wood and — perhaps that lovely earthenware vase? Then came the barking.

The Chicken Lady erupted from her bed at 6:18 a.m., spewing cuss words. She sprang to the window. She looked out.

She saw it all.

Thirty cows. In her yard. Meandering. Eating her pansies. And mooing. Plus, three police cars, complete with officers. Plus, one Animal Control officer. The humans, scratching their heads. The cows, blithely knocking over watering cans and clay pots and yard furniture. And neighborhood dogs urgently offering commentary, a kind of "Canine Bovine Report."

It was later learned that the cows had escaped from

Appleton Farms. And of all the fine folks in Ipswich whose yards they might have chosen for their meandering and munching and mooing, they chose the Chicken Lady. It seems these fugitive Flossies, pondering their options, apparently came to a consensus based on celebrity status.

"Where you wanna go?"

"I don't know, where do you wanna go?"

"We could go to the Chicken Lady's house."

"Oh, yeah! I read about her in the *Chronicle*. She's an animal-lover. She'll take us in."

And so it was.

Of course, Appleton Farms is a Trustees of Reservations property. As an enthusiastic member of the Trustees, I will not be surprised to receive a fundraising appeal in the near future, a "Padlocks for the Pasture" Campaign or some such.

Maybe they can get the Chicken Lady to offer a celebrity endorsement?

October 18, 2012

LIVE, FROM TOWN MEETING

(The "Special" One)

The May Town Meeting is required by law. The October Town Meeting is optional. But we always do it.

I sat in the front row again, with my pencil and sketchpad. Names withheld to protect the, uh, innocent....

126

130

MUOD 6
30000 10
43560 14

G'NIGHT!

133

COPING WITH THE
IPSWICH ITCH

I was probably crazy (the mosquito said) to come back here to Ipswich this year, after all that West Nile craziness last year. The mason jar imprisonments. The humiliating lab tests. The false accusations. (Yes, we took blood from school children. But we have no DNA connection to vampires. None!) Plus, may I just say, it was extremely hurtful to deal with the numerous put-downs of my home state of New Jersey.

After the trauma, and after we finally staggered back home, things actually went from bad to worse. Our family struggled. My children had nightmares about Board of Health interrogations. My wife never recovered emotionally; before long, she could only suck a pint a day. Ultimately she packed up the larvae and left for her mother's swamp in Morristown.

I was devastated, of course — and her lawyer saw to it that she got just about everything, right down to our Red Cross membership.

But life goes on. And maybe a part of me wanted to redeem the Ipswich nightmare. To prove to myself that I could conquer this town.

So yeah, I came back. Hooked up with the mosquito community. Tried to really get my nose into this place.

It wasn't easy. You upright mammals may have enjoyed the Ipswich summer, with all those dry, sunny days. But we were dying. Bored out of our wits. No place to go for, you know, recreation. Procreation, actually.

Mosquitoes can't live in a dry town. We need moisture, even more than humans do. We're very sensitive to chafing. You don't like a dry, scratchy kiss, do you? Well, imagine your whole six-millimeter-long nose feeling like that.

To you, it's just a slimy puddle along the shady side of your house. But to a mosquito, it's a water bed with a

pink lotus candle burning nearby. 2012, however, was not to be the Summer of Insect Love. Instead, Ipswich offered up a world-class drought, thank you very much.

It was impossible. You zip into a bar, you meet a nice-looking *Culiseta longiareolata* with a fine, sleek proboscis, maybe have a couple of drinks, get a little buzz to go with your buzz — but then: frustration. You take her to that one really good pothole on Linebrook Road: It's bone-dry. You whirr over to Old Town Hall, where a break in the gutter lets the rain cut a nice, juicy trough in the gravel: Now it's like a little slice of Arizona. You hope you'll get lucky in the curve of a throwaway tire out behind that one house on Greens Point Road, but no. It's so parched it's wrinkled, like a black rubber prune. "If you can't find anyplace we can go," she whines, "just take me home." The whole evening, ruined, for lack of a single, simple muck-hole.

And then, as if "local warming" wasn't enough, you had to go all SWAT team on us and spew bug-strangling poison gas into the air. I'm amazed, to tell you the truth, that humans put up with this stuff. It stinks! As if it's not barbarian enough to try and asphyxiate us, but for crying out loud, how do you stand the smell of that gunk? I'll just tell you the truth: When the gassing begins, we mosquitoes hold our breath — partly for the sake of survival, sure, but mostly to avoid the stench. At least sometimes you're clueless enough to dispense the toxins from airplanes — think that's impressive, do you? Since we actually live on the ground, it's those trucks doing their drive-by discharges that terrify us the most. Please, people. Can't we all just get along?

I want to say once and for all, I have nothing to do with West Nile. My family immigrated to Jersey from east of the Nile. Way east. Practically the Sinai. I don't blame you for not liking the Westies. We hated them when I was growing up. However, to be honest, this was mostly because they always creamed us at water polo.

Anyway, it's autumn. Ipswich seems to be getting moist again. We'll only have a few more days mild enough for me to get out and about. So let a skeeter alone, will ya?

November 21, 2012

GOOD LORD, It's IPSWICH

I bring, for my belov-ed home,
This brief Thanksgiving prayer and pome.
The only problem is that I'm
Still searching for a word to rhyme
With "Ipswich."

I want to sing the praises of
This little burg I've come to love —

Its quirks, its kinks, its oddities.
A word to rhyme, though, if you please,
With "Ipswich."

I thank Thee, Lord, for letting me
Enjoy our Town menagerie:
The clams, the greenheads, fisher cats,
The deer, the squirrels, and now, the rats
Of Ipswich.

For Masconomet, I give thanks
That he allowed us on these banks
And didn't squawk, nor get deranged,
When "Agawam" the white man changed
To "Ipswich."

We give Thee thanks for William Paine.
We give Thee thanks for Mr. Crane.
We give Thee thanks for all who so
Ungrudgingly gave land, and dough,
To Ipswich.

Our thanks Thou didst protect us through
The Feoffees' morphing, Old to New.
We thank Thee that it's over. Oh,
We thank Thee, Lord! The lawyers, though,
Thank Ipswich.

I praise Thee for Town Meeting, Lord,
Where citizens, in one accord,
With never even one dissent,
Advance the noble government
Of Ipswich.

We had an opening, a lack.
Bob Markel left; would not come back.
But Thou providedst, graciously,
A new T.M. to lovingly
Run Ipswich.

For this, we humbly bow to Thee:
Today, Town Hall is candle-free.
Town Manager hath set us straight —
Hath kept us from incinerat-
Ing Ipswich.

Of restaurant restrooms left unclean,
Our risk could not have been foreseen.
Thou moved our Board of Health to quiz 'em
So none might suffer botulism
In Ipswich.

We thank Thee that Thou art most pleas-ed
Not to let us be diseas-ed;
Rather, West Nile to allay,
Thou givest fumes that we may spray
On Ipswich.

Let all Creation sing for joy:
MacAlpine Thou didst not destroy
When from his Schwinn he tried to soar
From Boxford halfway back, or more,
To Ipswich.

Our Chicken Lady suffered long.
She suffered much. Thou made her strong,
That many hurdles she might clear

To make it safe for chickens here
In Ipswich.

Thou knewest how I'd love this place:
A village worthy of embrace.
Not Hamilton, not Topsfield. No.
Not Essex. And — thank God — we're so
Not Rowley.

About this year, I reminisce,
And thank Thee, Lord, for all of this,
And humbly pray for more good times —
Plus, if Thou couldst, a word that rhymes
With "Ipswich."

CREDIT DUE

One must bow to the individuals who labor valiantly, silently, in the background of any great book. I can't be referring to *this* book, of course, because this is not necessarily a "great" book. It's a silly book, essentially. But any book, good or bad, has individuals who labor valiantly, silently, in the background of it, and this book is no exception.

My wife **Kristina Brendel** serves as "first reader" for every column I produce. Sometimes she comes staggering agape from her office, drained of color. This is a clue. She has probably been reading my latest first draft. Kristina has endured admirably for more than a quarter-century as my frontline editor, in which capacity she has frequently saved me from myself. And spared the sensibilities of countless readers in the process.

I thank **Dan MacAlpine**, editor of the *Ipswich Chronicle*, who graciously invited me to this "columnist" role, and thereafter patiently tolerated me. After Dan's horrific bicycle accident on Labor Day, from which he is still recovering, managing editor **Janet Mackay-Smith** took over Brendel-babysitting duties, and has been remarkably serene throughout.

Finally, at the level of the nitty and the gritty, we come to the incomparable copy editor **Sarah Christine Jones**, of Copley, Ohio, who pores over the text through her editorial microscope. It can be said that she is a much younger and much more beautiful Madame Curie, searching not for radioactive isotopes but for poisonous punctuation, contaminated capitalization, and worst of all, leprous leaps of logic. Sarah eschews mere financial reward; she's above all that. Sarah Christine Jones serves for the cause. For the book. For the reader. And, ultimately, for the sake of laying her eyes on this single, monstrously overwrought paragraph of thanks.

DougBrendel.com

LET US CONNECT

Doug's contact info is at DougBrendel.com.
More about his columns: Outsidah.com.
Doug's ministry in the former USSR is NewThing.net.
His wife Kristina owns Time & Tide Fine Art in Ipswich, which is TimeAndTideFineArt.com.
Please contact us. It's lonely in outer Linebrook.

The material in this book is just Doug Brendel's. He writes as a volunteer for the *Ipswich Chronicle*, so anything in this book that also appeared in the *Chronicle* is Doug's responsibility. Don't blame the poor newspaper, for Pete's sake.

This book also has no official connection whatsoever to GateHouse Media, the *Ipswich Chronicle*'s parent company. Doug, however, unofficially reveres GateHouse, and does everything he can to keep them happy. Within reason.

Also, please note: *No clams were fried in the printing of this book.*

www.DougBrendel.com